MW00628048

Praise for *Driv*

"Joe Giglio is no newcomer to innovative thinking. I have read his work on privatization and transportation since the 1980s. In his new book, *Driving Questions*, don't expect to ride in the passenger seat. Joe puts the reader squarely behind the wheel in an insightful ride though the problems facing America's transportation system. Hold on. The ride's not pretty...but there is light at the end of the tunnel." **– Tom Beasley, former CEO, Chairman, and founder of Corrections Corporation of America**

"Joe Giglio knows how to close big deals and how to solve big problems. America can't solve its infrastructure crisis without listening to people like him."
– Governor Mitch Daniels of Indiana

"An insightful look into the strategic issues at a critical point for our transportation system." **– Mark Florian, Managing Director, Goldman, Sachs & Co.**

"Joe Giglio has pulled no punches nor spared any sacred cows in calling for a new transportation vision. He raises good questions – questions that, whether you agree with him or not, need to be addressed."
– Robert L. Darbelnet, President and Chief Executive Officer, AAA

"Another great read by Dr. Giglio. Strategy and transportation....you mean they go together? Professor Giglio is a true visionary in solving transportation issues. *Driving Questions* is a must read for anyone who is interested in driving home real solutions."
– Tom R. Skancke, Commissioner, National Surface Transportation Policy and Revenue Study Commission

"Dr. Giglio's expansive and incisive knowledge is clearly demonstrated by the important discussion he leads throughout this book. Much of his insight amounts to 'the Emperor has no clothes' in regard to traditional transportation thinking and deed. Dr. Giglio leads a discussion our nation must have, and soon."
– Pete Rahn, Director of the Missouri Department of Transportation

"With the skills of a keen historian and an even keener strategist, Professor Giglio takes on three daunting tasks: unraveling the interests and agendas that have knotted up transportation debates for decades and brought the nation to a crisis point, itemizing the costs if we do not confront the core issues, and presenting a clear, concise framework to move the country forward. That's a heroic agenda, laid out with a personal flair that is all his own." **– James Stergios, Executive Director, Pioneer Institute**

"Professor Giglio's *Mobility* book outlined the transportation issues facing America. This book raises the questions we must address. It is entertaining, informative and a must read for transportation professionals." **– Patricia Abbate, CEO, Citizens for Rail Safety, Inc.**

"Professor Giglio takes a unique and refreshing approach to dealing with strategy and transportation. He prepares the reader to confront the questions and consider the answers about building and financing a 21st- century integrated surface transportation system."
– Alan G. MacDonald, Executive Director, Massachusetts Business Roundtable

"Dr. Giglio's voice is an important one at a critical time in our transportation history. He weighs in by going right to the heart of the basic questions we need to consider in order to create a transportation system that will meet our future needs."
– Neil Schuster, President and CEO, ITSA- Intelligent Transportation Society of America

"Professor Giglio provides a road map for policy makers to develop sound strategies to fund and repair the nation's transportation infrastructure."
– David Fink, President, Pan Am Railways

"In a few pages, Giglio asks the hard questions about our nation's vital transportation system. For a system on medical alert, he challenges all of us to think bigger, act smarter – and get involved in helping to chart the next 100 years for our country's critical transportation infrastructure and services." **– Beverly A. Scott, PhD., General Manager and CEO, Sacramento Regional Transit District**

"Once again, Professor Giglio has looked at how we should deliver transportation services in the U.S. through the lens of integration and alignment – the alignment of vision, funding, modes, and the interests of users. In the game of transportation, he sees the entire board and beyond." **– Patrick D. Jones, Executive Director, IBTTA**

"A thought-provoking critical mass of information and ideas that will certainly enable a spirited debate and sensible solutions to our emerging national transportation crisis."
– Michael C. Ascher, P.E., retired President, MTA Bridges and Tunnels

"Clearly identifies the issues related to providing an efficient and effective multi-modal transportation system and is on target with the strategies and partnerships needed to make this vision a reality."
– Hope Andrade, Commissioner of the Texas Transportation Commission

"A brilliant, inspirational book that challenges us to a higher performance plane. Joe Giglio's insight into transportation strategy development and customer focus is motivating!" **– Jack Lettiere, former Secretary of Transportation in New Jersey**

"From FDR's 'War Plan Orange' to defeat the Japanese Imperial Navy, to management guru Peter Drucker's admonition that the purpose of enterprise is to create 'customers,' Joe Giglio has challenged us with the urgent need to develop a national transportation strategy. To do so he says we need to focus more on 'content,' and less on 'form.' I believe he is right in that distinction, and right to point to the need for a new national strategy." **– John Horsley, Executive Director of the American Association of State Highway and Transportation Officials (AASHTO)**

"Professor Giglio 'tells it like it is': how we have lost our way in being able to formulate a transportation strategy for this nation. Using an insightful model from the American military's successful World War II strategy in the Pacific; he skillfully and colorfully guides us toward learning how we can determine what we need and why." **– Martin E. Robins, Senior Fellow and former Director of the Bloustein Center at Rutgers University**

"Dr. Giglio brings clarity to approaching complex problems that makes one think in fresh ways about how to solve them. With this book he does it again." **– Bill Millar, President of the American Public Transportation Association**

"As with his previous book *Mobility* this book is funny, provocative, insightful and refreshingly independent-minded. We need a book like this to achieve a workable surface transportation strategy going forward." **– Jane Garvey, Chairman of the Transportation Practice APCO Worldwide and former Administrator of FAA**

"Professor Giglio has, again, led the reader on an intriguing journey. There is a compelling argument for a 'national strategy' for the US; however, Professor Giglio has framed the debate with historical examples separating the 'strategic' context from 'tactical' approaches most common today. He outlines the probable rose of the various 'publics' (i.e., federal, state/regional and local governments) and the various models of conceivable public-public and public-private partnerships. The book should be required reading for public officials and private sector leaders for shaping the next strategic plan for our nation's transportation system." **– C. Michael Walton, Ph.D., P.E., Ernest H. Cockrell Centennial Chair in Engineering at the University of Texas at Austin**

"Dr. Giglio presents an interesting assessment of the strategy behind the planning and implementation of our nation's transportation systems. He describes how reliance on narrowly focused and short-term solutions has prevented us, as a nation, from following our own advice and establishing a coherent vision of transportation. I have no doubt that the questions he raises and his analysis will give pause to consider." **– Lawrence Chiarelli, P.E., Esq., Industry Professor and Associate Director of the Center of Construction Management Technology, Polytechnic University**

"Once again, Joe Giglio is asking questions and urging us to stretch beyond current thinking for the answers. It's good to know that 'we' includes Joe." **– Susan A. Buse, CFO, North Texas Tollway Authority and First Vice President of IBTTA.**

Also by Joseph M. Giglio

Mobility: America's Transportation Mess and How to Fix It (Hudson Institute, 2005)

Fast Lane to the Future: The Privatization Route (Hudson Institute, 1996)

Driving Questions

Developing a National Transportation Vision

Joseph M. Giglio

HUDSON INSTITUTE
Washington, D.C.

JOSEPH M. GIGLIO

Mr. Giglio's unique background in business, public policy and finance is rooted in his experience in Wall Street, in management consulting, in government service and in academia.

Mr. Giglio served as the Special Advisor to the Office of the Secretary of Transportation. He is also the Vice Chairman of the Hudson Institute, a leading public policy organization in Washington D.C. In addition, Mr. Giglio teaches strategic management at the Graduate School of Business at Northeastern University in Boston. He has served as full-time faculty since September 1997. During the three years between 1998 and 2000 he was selected as the outstanding professor at the Graduate School of Business.

Mr. Giglio has served as Executive Vice President at Smith Barney, President of Chase Municipal Securities, and as Senior Managing Director at Bear, Stearns & Co. Inc. The American Banker recognized Mr. Giglio as the "Outstanding Investment Banker" for several years. Also, he served as Chairman of Apogee Research Inc. Prior to going to Wall Street, Mr. Giglio held a series of senior management positions with the Federal Government as well as the City and State of New York.

Mr. Giglio served as Chairman of President Reagan's National Council on Public Works Improvement, which released its report "Fragile Foundations" in 1988. He also chaired the U.S. Senate Budget Commission on Innovative Financing of Infrastructure from 1983-1986. From 2000, Mr. Giglio served as Chairman of the Board of Directors for the Intelligent Transportation Society of America (ITSA), a federally charted advisory committee addressing public and private sector technology applications. He served as Vice Chairman of ITSA from 1998-1999, and is a former board member of the Massachusetts Higher Education Financing Authority. Also, he is the former Chairman of the Public-Private Division of the American Road and Transportation Builders Association.

Mr. Giglio was appointed to the board of the Special Commission on Transportation Finance and the Health and Education Facilities Authority by Gov. Romney. Additionally, Mr. Giglio is adjunct faculty at Polytechnic University in New York City.

Mr. Giglio sits on the board of a number of private corporations and has been a prolific author on finance and transportation public policy. He holds a B.A. degree from Rutgers University, an M.P.A. degree from New York University, an M.B.A. degree from Columbia Business School and a Ph.D. degree from Northeastern University.

ISBN: 1-55813-154-X

For more information about obtaining additional copies of this or other
Hudson Institute publications, please contact Hudson's website at
www.hudson.org/bookstore or call toll free: 1-888-554-1325.

For media and speaking engagement purposes, contact Hudson Institute
at 202-974-2400, or email at info@hudson.org.

About Hudson Institute:
Hudson Institute is a non-partisan policy research organization dedicated
to innovative research and analysis that promotes global security, prosperity,
and freedom. We challenge conventional thinking and help manage strategic
transitions to the future through interdisciplinary and collaborative studies
in defense, international relations, economics, culture, science, technology,
and law. Through publications, conferences, and policy recommendations,
we seek to guide global leaders in government and business.

For more information, visit www.hudson.org

To Staying New

ACKNOWLEDGMENTS

For starters, I owe a high debt of gratitude to the Fab Five, who have played seminal roles in motivating and intellectually inspiring this work. My heartfelt thanks go to Martin Capper, President, Mark IV IVHS Division, Michael Doyle, CEO, Econolite Group, Inc., Howard (Butch) Eley, CEO, Infrastructure Corporation of America, Jeff Held, V.P., Corporate Development, Quixote Corporation and Harry Voccola, Senior Vice President, NAVTEQ.

I am also grateful to the College of Business, Northeastern University for funding and research support and the Hudson Institute for giving me a platform to introduce and develop my ideas.

Of course, all errors and misjudgments are entirely my own. Feel free to correct me but not publicly.

Contents

Good teaching is more a giving of right questions than a giving of right answers. – JOSEPF ALBERS

Prelude:

STARTING OVER

First a confession.

This book isn't a product of the usual magisterial isolation in an academic setting where time beats to its own stately metronome. Instead, it grew out of real-world testimony about improving transportation in the United States that I presented before the National Surface Transportation Policy and Revenue Study Commission in Dallas on September 20, 2006.

The testimony's purpose was to set forth a framework for defining certain strategic questions about transportation in the United States. It seemed to me we had to address these questions before we got caught up in the next round of debate about such tactical issues as appropriate levels of funding, how to restore the rapidly-depleting balances of the Federal Transportation Trust Fund, and new ways to pay for transportation improvements.

So the book tries to flesh out the important points in the testimony, respond to questions it generated among Commission members and others, and clarify the three strategic questions that formed its core.

To avoid any confusion, these questions are:

- *What should the nation's transportation system look like in the future?*
- *What options do we have for transforming the existing system to match this vision?*
- *What resources are available to carry out these options?*

These are *strategic* questions because the answers to them will determine the shape of any tactical programs we develop to improve the nation's transportation system. And they still remain unanswered. Mainly because we have yet to ask them in a properly serious way.

Strategy is a million-dollar word with multiple meanings that can lead to all kinds of confusion. There seems to be at least lip-service agreement that a superior strategy is behind every successful enterprise, so it's something we have to take seriously. But beyond this, most discussions of strategy seem to degenerate into vagueness and irrelevancies.

Is strategy some MBA-type's interpretation of elaborate Excel spreadsheets full of numbers that claim to define the shape of an enterprise's future? Is it a carbon copy of something that hindsight shows worked well for another enterprise at another point in time? Is it the ad hoc play calling of a CEO whose gut instincts (or maybe just pure luck) have made him a Wall Street favorite so far? Is it solely the product of stained-glass rational thought uncontaminated by the hurly-burly of the real world? Is it kitchen-sink experimentation? Is it a finished painting to be worshiped at arm's length? Is it something we fall back on when all else fails?

Those of us who read books on "business strategy" often come away with the uneasy sense that each author has defined the term in self-serving ways to support whatever particular management shtick he happens to be promoting. In this context, strategy may seem like nothing more than an impressive label pasted on an author's pet idea to boost sales of his or her book.

Fortunately, strategy is far more than a simple-minded buzzword. It has an impressive intellectual pedigree that's many centuries old.

Originally, it was developed by the military to answer the question "How do we use armies to further a nation's interests?" But as civilization matured and other kinds of large enterprises came to play important roles in developing societies, strategy moved beyond the purely military arena.

The Roman Catholic Church, the East India Company during the early period of Third World colonizing by European nations, the railroads and other industrial corporations spawned by the Industrial Revolution, all adopted the military discipline of strategy in one form or another to help themselves grow and gain power. In the process, it became apparent that effective strategy had to embody an ongoing process for adapting to rapidly changing environments. How else could the Roman Catholic Church have become the world's largest, richest, and most influential religious enterprise?

In some cases, an awareness of strategic potential has even given birth to large enterprises that didn't previously exist. This happened during the 1930s when a rag-tag collection of feuding criminal gangs in major American cities got shaped into a smoothly functioning cartel that became an important national industry known popularly (if inaccurately) as "The Mafia."

This cartel was largely the inspiration of Manhattan gambler Arnold Rothstein and Chicago gang leader Johnny Torrio. Both were visionary strategic thinkers who lamented the enormous potential profits from bootlegging and other activities they saw being left on the table as individual gangs wasted too much of their energy on pointless blood feuds. And in the best tradition of practical capitalism, they became convinced that cooperation would yield more benefits than competition.

So under the aggressive leadership of such protégés like Lucky Luciano, Meyer Lansky, Frank Costello, and Longy Zwillman, the traditional gangs were hammered into large groups of cooperative enterprises. Among the initiated, this crowd was called the Kosher Nostra. Which proceeded to parcel out business territories, create a national board of directors and internal enforcement arms like Murder Incorporated, buy comprehensive protection from local politicians and police departments, and expand their activities into a wider variety of illegal and quasi-legal activities. And became hugely profitable as a result.

One of history's most successful examples of real world strategy-in-action is the U.S. Navy's War Plan Orange. This was a detailed game plan for defeating Japan in the event that its geopolitical rivalry with the U.S. after 1900 should lead to war.

During the forty years prior to World War II, the specifics of War Plan Orange went through more than two dozen revisions to adopt to realities like evolving naval technology, the ebbs and flows of diplomatic relations between the two nations, internal power struggles in Japan for control of its government, changing ideas within the U.S. government about offensive vs. defensive stances with respect to Japan, and the role of the U.S. in conflicts among its major European trading partners.

But throughout, War Plan Orange's underlying vision remained intact.

- **War would begin with a surprise attack by Japan. Probably against the U.S. colonies of the Philippines or Guam in the Western Pacific, acquired as a result of the Spanish-American War.**

- **Japan would promptly invade the Philippines. The U.S. Army garrison there (which couldn't be reinforced) would fight a delaying action to buy as much time as possible for the U.S. Navy to get its act together for a counter-offensive, and to deny the use of Manila Bay as a base for the Imperial Japanese Navy.**

- **The U.S. Navy would steam across the Central Pacific (establishing temporary supply bases on various convenient islands along the way) to seek out and destroy the Imperial Japanese Navy in one or more climactic sea battles in the waters between the Philippines and Japan.**

- **With its navy destroyed, import-dependent Japan would be subject to a total blockade and siege by the U.S. fleet that would cripple its ability to carry on the war requiring its government to enter into peace negotiations. The result would be Japan's acceptance of U.S. dominance in the Pacific Rim.**

Those of you who are familiar with the history of World War II in the Pacific know that this is pretty much what happened. But like all good strategies, War Plan Orange was able to be modified along the way to respond to unanticipated events. For example:

- Japan's surprise attack on December 7, 1941 actually came against Pearl Harbor (though it was followed up within twelve hours by attacks on the Philippines, Guam, and Wake Island). The Pearl Harbor attack crippled the battleships that the U.S. Navy had always regarded as its primary offensive force. So under the clear-eyed leadership of Pacific Fleet commander Admiral Chester Nimitz, the Navy turned to task forces built around its aircraft carriers. But as it turned out, the aircraft carrier became the primary naval offensive weapon in the Pacific War in the hands of gifted admirals like Ray Spruance and Bill Halsey. Even after the battleships crippled at Pearl Harbor were replaced by brand new battleships (especially the superlative *Iowa* class) that could run rings around anything in the Imperial Japanese Navy.

- For political reasons, President Franklin Roosevelt had to establish a Southwestern Pacific command for General Douglas MacArthur (who had botched the defense of the Philippines and was evacuated to Australia). This had nothing to do with War Plan Orange and was entirely tangential. But MacArthur was a particular favorite of Republicans in the U.S. Congress, and Roosevelt needed their cooperation to pursue his larger agenda of "Beat Germany First" in partnership with the U.K. and the Soviet Union. Fortunately, Roosevelt's success in turning the U.S. economy into an overwhelming "Arsenal of Democracy" after his 1940 reelection meant that War Plan Orange's Central Pacific emphasis was never compromised by any shortages of fighting men or equipment.

- But even after the U.S. Navy destroyed the Imperial Japanese Navy in two devastating sea-warfare Super Bowls (the Battle of the Philippine Sea in June 1944 and the Battle of Leyte Gulf in October 1944), Japan's government showed no signs of being willing to enter peace negotiations. It was controlled by army generals whose Samurai culture (like Hitler's mad passion for a Wagnerian Gotterdammerung) dictated national suicide in the name of the Emperor as a better alternative to the humiliation of a Western-style negotiated peace.

- So during 1945, War Plan Orange had to be amended to pursue a four-pronged endgame. This included the originally planned sea- and air-blockade, which rapidly brought Japan to the verge of starvation; a massive aerial bombing campaign by B-29s that burned down 69 Japanese cities and culminated in the August atomic-bomb raids against Hiroshima and Nagasaki; preparations for a land invasion that would have wiped out a significant proportion of Japan's population; and Joseph Stalin's promise to turn the frightening power of the Red Army loose against Japan. As it happened, Japan's Emperor finally woke up to the fact that his own semi-sacred position as Head of State was in danger as Japan moved ever closer to a German-style national collapse. So he directed the government to seek peace. Which came on August 15, 1945.

War Plan Orange guided the U.S. to victory over Japan barely three years and eight months after the Pearl Harbor attack. This was less than half the time the U.S. spent in Vietnam, and shorter than the current Iraq conflict. It was obviously a sound strategy to begin with. Equally important, it was flexible enough to roll with the punches from unexpected events that planners weren't able to anticipate. That makes it a textbook example of strategic planning at its best.

And it illustrates why a study of military history provides essential background for those attempting to develop effective strategies for transportation and other large enterprises. Without this background, they're like techno-wannabes trying to do engineering without having studied physics.

Meanwhile, let's be clear and stipulate without hesitation that having a strategy means knowing *what* we're trying to accomplish, *how* we can accomplish it, and *what resources* we need to accomplish it.

Example from War Plan Orange:

- ***What* was the U.S. seeking to accomplish?**
  Persuade an aggressive Japan to accept U.S. influence in the Western Pacific and the Pacific Rim.

- ***How* could the U.S. accomplish this?**
  Defeat the Imperial Japanese Navy in one or more classic sea battles so it could impose a close-in siege of Japan by sea and air forces until Japan capitulated.

- ***What resources* would the U.S. need to accomplish this?**
  A first-class naval fleet that was larger and more powerful than the Imperial Japanese Navy. Plus temporary naval bases strung out across the Central Pacific to support this fleet. Plus an air force that could bomb Japanese cities during the siege from island bases near Japan that had been seized by U.S. Marines.

Right now, we probably have the surface transportation network we deserve. Especially in view of our decades-long unwillingness to maintain it adequately and invest in it properly.

But there's a nagging sense that we don't have the transportation network we need to support a decent level of economic growth. This means that any tactical transportation improvement programs we may have (either in practice or in shelves full of elaborate studies) lack essential soundness.

Therefore, whatever funding gaps and other shortcomings we think exist for carrying out these tactical programs are speculative at best. How could they be otherwise when we haven't yet developed a sound strategy for turning the present transportation system into what the nation needs? We have to stop trying to put the cart before the horse and start over.

In other words, we should stop concentrating on form and start focusing on content.

Form is concerned with the *tactical specifics* of doing things. It deals with such questions as:

- ***Should state governments lease their existing toll highways to private consortiums and use the up-front cash they receive to fund construction of road and rail projects that have been sitting on the shelf due to lack of funds?***

- ***Should state governments implement roadway pricing on key links of their highway systems to make them self-supporting enterprises and thereby assure adequate funds for their on-going maintenance, capital reconstruction, and expansion?***

- ***Should state governments enter into partnerships with private firms to build and operate new self-supporting road and rail projects?***

- *Should state governments try to leverage future federal grants by converting them into income streams to pay debt service on bonds they issue today to fund capital construction on new road and rail projects?*

- *Should states use federal grant funds to capitalize Infrastructure banks that make revolving loans to transportation projects?*

- *Should government establish objective, enforceable performance standards against which transportation providers can be held accountable as EPA has done for air quality?*

These are all reasonable questions. But they're meaningless until we know *what* we're trying to accomplish with transportation. This is the *content* issue, and we must deal with it before we can address the issue of *form*.

We should begin by answering four key questions:

- *What is the main purpose of surface transportation systems?*

- *What resources are available to make these systems better?*

- *How can we best use these resources?*

- *How do we measure our success in making transportation systems better?*

These strategic questions have remained unanswered far too long.

Mainly because those of us in the transportation community rarely ask them in thoughtful ways. And it's time we started doing so.

My middle name may not be Elijah, but I would like to outline some thinking that may help us frame these questions in ways that can generate meaningful answers.

What is the Purpose of Transportation?

The answer to this question should be obvious enough once we cut through the tangled underbrush of wooly-headed ideas that pass for received wisdom in too many discussions of transportation. Stripped to its essentials:

The basic purpose of transportation is to support the nation's economy.

One of the unavoidable facts of life is that economic activity generates demand for moving people and goods. The more economic activity we have, the greater is this demand. Therefore the capacity of our roadway, freight rail, and public transit systems must be sufficient to accommodate this demand. Otherwise the nation's level of economic activity is going to be less than it could be. And we'll all be poorer as a result.

A growing economy is what keeps America strong and prosperous. And effective transportation is one of the most important underpinnings for a growing economy.

In other words, transportation is a *derived* demand rather than a *direct* demand. It's a natural consequence of our direct demand for higher incomes, greater economic prosperity, and a higher quality of life.

Example from War Plan Orange:

- **The size and composition of the U.S. Pacific fleet represented a derived demand. It was a natural consequence of the U.S.'s direct demand for a dominating position in the Western Pacific.**

Because transportation is a derived demand, we don't find many Americans sitting around kitchen tables or in corporate board rooms discussing it. Or listing it as a major national issue in public opinion polls. Effective transportation may be a silent prerequisite for achieving many of the national goals Americans like to discuss. But it lacks inherent sex appeal and is therefore easy to ignore. Just as AIDS was easy to ignore before tennis star Arthur Ashe publicly announced that he had contracted it from a blood transfusion, and proceeded to die from it with all the grace and style he displayed in his memorable backhand.

This may help to explain the appeal of arguments by anti-highway types, who often masquerade as "concerned environmentalists" in opposing as "self-defeating" many proposed transportation projects (especially roads) designed to address capacity shortfalls.

At the core of their arguments is a concept they like to call *induced* demand. This means that a new road or other transportation facility will simply encourage more people to make more trips until eventually its new capacity is saturated. Leaving us right back where we started.

This is logical enough as far as it goes. But anti-highway types imply that the new trips generated by induced demand have no economic significance. They're simply idle joy riding, in other words. Trips we could easily do without.

However the overwhelming proportions of these new induced demand trips have considerable economic significance. People making these trips are doing so to buy or sell goods and services. To produce or consume in ways that weren't previously possible.

In other words, these trips generate new economic activity that couldn't otherwise take place. Therefore the induced demand potential of building new capacity for moving people by road and rail means that such projects don't merely fill a passive role of accommodating existing economic activity. They can play an active role in stimulating new economic activity. As such, they become important tools for growing the economy.

Of course, not everyone regards economic growth as a good thing. Those who subscribe to a Marie Antoinette view of society may find it inconveniently disruptive. Especially if it provides opportunities for the "wrong kind of people" to rise in the world, to realize their full human potential through hard work, to enjoy decent living standards, and to share in the economic and social benefits that were formerly monopolized by those who were born into the "right families."

The ranks of anti-transportation types are filled with these "let-them-eat-cake" acolytes. Their numbers may not be great in percentage terms. But their influence can be enormous. And many of the lawyers among them have become experts at exploiting environmental regulations to entangle new transportation projects in dense thickets of litigation that can drag on for years. Until they've watered down the meaning of such projects into an exceedingly thin gruel. All part of their insistence on freezing in time an antiquated social status quo against the liberating power of anything that smacks of economic growth.

Needless to say, we can't blame all our transportation woes on these anti-transportation types. Especially when we've done so much to help them by failing to come up with sensible programs for assuring the kind of mobility our nation requires.

At least part of the problem may be that we have yet to develop a coherent strategic vision of what an effective system for moving people and goods by road and rail should look like. And not just for today but for half a century down the road.

Example from War Plan Orange:

- **U.S. control over the Philippines and Guam as a result of the Spanish-American War established the practical possibility that the U.S. could play a major role in the future of China and other Pacific Rim nations. But exploiting this possibility in the spirit of Manifest Destiny was likely to lead to serious rivalry with Japan.**

Developing a coherent vision for transportation requires that we look into the future to identify the kind of services that transportation systems must provide. Then we can work backwards to flesh out the details of the specific needs these systems must satisfy.

This involves two kinds of strategic activities.

- ***First: we must understand the external environment within which transportation systems function, both now and in the future.*** The external environment is what determines the demands placed on transportation systems. Evolutionary changes in this environment will affect future transportation demands. So we must position ourselves ahead of the curve to understand how these demands may evolve. This means that our analysis of the external environment should be an ongoing process.

- ***Second: we must know the details of the needs that transportation customers are willing to pay good money to have satisfied.*** We do this by conducting the right kind of market research. Inevitably, customer perceptions of their needs change over time as they respond to changes in the external environment. So market research must also be an ongoing process.

Note the repeated use of the term ongoing. This is no accident. Good strategy is never "finished" like a formal landscape painting. It's always a work-in-progress, just as War Plan Orange was. Therefore, we must always be scanning the horizon for new challenges to which our strategies have to respond.

Analyzing the Evolving Environment

Back in 1956, Elia Kazan celebrated the tradition-bound world of intercontinental goods movement in his Oscar-winning film, *On The Waterfront*. But who could have imagined that this world was on the verge of becoming as obsolete as the Marlon Brando character's boxing career?

Because 1956 was also the year that an entrepreneurial trucking magnate named Malcolm McLean first arranged to pack hundreds of individual crates of goods into a few large steel-containers that could quickly and efficiently be transferred by mechanical cranes between ocean-going ships and land-based trailer trucks without disturbing their contents. Quite a change from the age-old tradition of having large crews of dockworkers slowly move by hand each of these individual crates from ships to trucks and vice versa.

This marked the birth of a goods movement technology we now call *containerization*. By slashing the costs of moving goods from one part of the world to another, it made possible the huge growth in trans-global trade around the world. Today, a person in Kansas City can buy consumer goods mass-produced in China for a fraction of the price that his grandparents would have had to pay. And in the process, containerization totally transformed the infrastructure and operations of the ocean shipping and port industries.

We should remember that containerization wasn't the brainchild of either industry. It was initially conceived and developed by a visionary outsider who imposed it on reluctant ocean shipping and port operating firms that would have much preferred to keep on doing the same old things in the same old ways.

In other words, containerization became part of the external environment within which ocean shipping and port operations have to function. So these classic industries had to learn how to understand its implications for their businesses. We must do the same thing when it comes to the external environment within which transportation functions.

Example from War Plan Orange:

- **One key variable in the external environment affecting U.S. ambitions in the Far East was the geophysical reality of the vast Pacific Ocean. This was the only practical trade highway between Pacific Rim nations and the Western Hemisphere. So freedom of passage for commercial ships in the Pacific had to be secured and enforced by a strong fleet of U.S. warships.**

- **A second key variable was the fact that Japan was the most industrially advanced Asian nation. Understandably, Japan believed that it should play the leadership role in developing the Pacific Rim. This made rivalry and conflict with the U.S. inevitable.**

- **A third key variable was the rapid development of warship technology during the first two decades of the 20th century. This made each new class of warships much more effective than previous classes, which imposed very expensive naval construction programs on the U.S. and Japan.**

The key variables of the external environment for surface transportation conveniently group themselves into four broad categories: economic variables, demographic variables, technological variables, and socio-political variables.

Economic Variables

The most important of these variables are those involving trends in the growth of Gross Domestic Product (GDP) at the national level, plus at the state and local levels, plus within different industries. The GDP is how we measure the level of economic activity. Which is what creates the demand for moving people and goods.

Other economic variables include inflation, employment levels (in gross terms and as percentages of the total labor force), capital formation (by both the private and public sectors), and the government fiscal picture (federal, state, and local).

Demographic Variables

These variables concern people. Ultimately, it's people who produce the GDP. Who demand transportation of various kinds and in various quantities for various travel purposes. And who generate the financial resources to fund transportation systems. So we need to know:

- How many people will live in the United States at various points in the future?

- Where are they likely to live (by state, by local region within each state, and by multi-state regions like the East and West Coasts)?

- How many will live in single-person vs. multi-person households (with and without children)?

- How old will they be (it's no secret that the rising proportion of senior citizens will impose new mobility needs that we've never had to confront in the past)?

- How large will their incomes be (which helps to define how much they can pay for transportation)?

- How much education will they have (higher levels of education tend to make people more demanding and choosy about what they will pay for, and more willing to make use of new technologies)?

Demographics is a social science that can provide projections that tend to be closer to the physical sciences in terms of their precision and accuracy. So their projections are especially helpful in determining what the future will look like.

Technological Variables

Interestingly, the field of surface transportation is on the verge of becoming awash with new technology that may be just as transforming as containerization was for ocean shipping and port operations.

We already have new technologies for collecting roadway tolls without slowing the speeds of motorists, for measuring the average speeds and densities of traffic flows on roadway lanes at any given moment, and for pinpointing the location of buses and other public transportation vehicles on their routes.

But just over the horizon are technologies that have the potential for making transportation much safer and more efficient by:

- Providing instant communications between roadway operators and motor vehicles concerning bottlenecks up ahead and alternate routes.

- Preventing traffic accidents.

- Minimizing deaths, injuries, and collateral damage in accidents that can't be avoided.

- Monitoring the contents of goods movement containers moving by road, rail, and air without disrupting traffic flows.

But these new technologies can be as much curses as blessings unless we learn how to properly manage their transfers from the laboratory to the marketplace.

For example, we face the prospect of having to evaluate the pros and cons of implementing tolls on limited-access highways, and of entering into concession agreements with private firms to operate such highways. But how can we do this realistically until we understand the likely impact of new technologies on these highways down the road?

So we need as much information as possible about what these technologies are, how they work, what they can do, and what problems they pose.

Also, let's not forget that the design and use of any technological innovations must be customer-driven, not provider-driven. So obvious. Yet so often overlooked.

Socio-Political Variables

Identifying and evaluating these variables may often seem like exercises in pure futurism. But this doesn't mean that we should think of them as idle speculations. Even when the results of such evaluations may seem to lack the scientific precision of demographics, information about the form and content of these variables can be very important in helping us determine the future shape of the external environment.

Special emphasis should be given to the potential impact of the following socio-political issues:

- Continued increases in global trade (which stimulates further competition among nations and demands that we regard American transportation systems as links in world-wide travel chains rather than as stand-alone entities isolated and protected by national borders).

- More open policies regarding immigration (leading to a larger proportion of American residents being born abroad) rather than tighter policies (leading to a larger proportion of residents being native born).

- Growing political clout among increasingly numerous senior citizens. Who will insist that American society provide them with comfortable retirements, special treatment of their particular needs, and meaningful protection of their purchasing power after their working days are over.

- Continued decline in the willingness and ability of corporate America to provide its current and retired employees with the kind of social welfare services traditionally provided by national governments in Europe and elsewhere.

- Further replacement of traditional mass markets for goods and services by niche markets as consumer demand becomes more sophisticated and industry responds by "customizing" its production methods.

- People willing to "cram more living into each day" by making use of timesaving technologies like cell phones and the internet.

- More ethnic, income, and educational diversity in workplaces and markets.

- Single-person and no-children households becoming dominant household types.

- Rising concern for environmental issues and conservation of natural resources.

There's a vast amount of information already available about these four categories of variables. Our task is to turn this information into cogent scenarios detailing the likely patterns that define the future shape of the external environment for transportation.

But simply describing these scenarios is not enough. We also need to accommodate the key reality of uncertainty into each scenario. In the case of scenarios for future GDP growth, for example, we want to be able to tell the public (not to mention each other) that:

> *"There are nine chances out of ten that national GDP growth during the next ten years will average at least X percent per year. And three chances out of four that it will average at least Y percent (larger than X). And one chance out of two that it will average at least Z percent (larger than Y)."*

Once we understand the evolving environment, we can move on to the task of developing a serious strategic vision of what an effective transportation system should look like.

The "Ideal Model" Benchmark

As this vision takes shape, we may find it helpful to sketch out some of the transportation possibilities that occur to us along the way. These wouldn't necessarily be firm proposals that anyone expects to implement. Instead, they would be illustrations of the vision's potential under ideal circumstances. As such, they can provide benchmarks against which we can measure the effectiveness of actual proposals that emerge further down the road.

Here's an example.

Once upon a time (way back during the first decade of the 21st century), the government of a major industrial state had become concerned about increasing traffic congestion and other transportation problems in its largest metropolitan region. It feared that failure to address these problems in a serious manner could limit future economic growth in the region.

This would have significant repercussions throughout the state. And since the nation's twenty largest metropolitan regions generate more than half its GDP (even with only about forty percent of the U.S. population), the national consequences could be very troubling.

- **After due consideration of various alternatives, the state government created a new, independent commercial enterprise called Metro Transport to take over responsibility for the metropolitan region's deteriorating and increasingly costly roadway system. This included its limited-access expressways, its boulevards and other important arterials that connected with the expressways, and its many miles of local access streets.**

- **Metro Transport was charged with being fully self-supporting. It did this by using state-of-the-art electronic toll collection technology to charge motorists mileage-based tolls for travel on the region's heavily used expressways.**

- **These tolls were set at rates designed to generate sufficient revenue to cover the costs of operating and maintaining** the roadway system to state-of-the-art standards, maintaining it at something close to showroom-new condition, replacing or restoring worn-out links and other facilities in a timely fashion, expanding lane capacity as needed to accommodate growing travel demand, and producing a reasonable return on its invested capital.

- As an independent enterprise that was supported entirely by the motorists who use its roadways, Metro Transport received no tax subsidies of any kind. This freed it from dependence on federal, state, and local motor vehicle fuel taxes (which were no longer collected in the region). And from annual appropriations in the hard-pressed budgets of the local governments in the region's central city and its five suburban counties. Not to mention capital construction grants from the federal government.

- Electronic toll collection enabled Metro Transport to vary its mileage-based toll rates on short notice. Therefore, it could use such differential pricing to induce some trips to be made during times of the day when travel demand is lower. Or to be made on roadway links that were less heavily used. It can even offer motorists using toll expressways money-back performance guarantees in the best customer-oriented tradition of enlightened consumer product corporations. Reducing toll rates proportionally if traffic speeds fell below the posted minimum.

- The effect of rationalizing travel in this way was to increase the functional efficiency of the region's roadway system by

raising its aggregate daily vehicle throughput. The result was the same as expanding capacity by adding new lanes, but without the high cost and other problems associated with roadway construction.

The basic idea behind the hypothetical construct called Metro Transport came from a review of Hong Kong, whose aggressive embrace of free-market capitalism has helped its nearly seven million residents to enjoy one of the highest per-capita levels of Gross Domestic Product in the world.

Over the years, Hong Kong's regional government has established and capitalized various commercial corporations to carry out important economic development functions. These include building and operating its subway system, its commuter rail system, and its international airport complex – all of which are widely regarded as among the best in the world. Also included is Hong Kong Disneyland, a successful amusement theme park.

This concept of government-based venture capitalism has even extended to selling minority ownership shares in these corporations to private investors through Hong Kong's stock market once they've established good track records for profitability. In the best traditions of private sector venture capitalism, doing this enables Hong Kong's government to recover some of its originally invested capital and put it to work in new development projects to help the region's economy grow.

- **To raise some of the capital funds needed to restore and improve the roadway system, Metro Transport sold equity ownership shares to private investors. These investors were attracted by the promise of secure dividends from Metro Transport's toll revenues. And under properly structured**

limited partnership arrangements, such dividends were partially sheltered from federal income tax liability by having Metro Transport pass through to investors its deductions for debt interest and tax depreciation. This further enhanced the after-tax value of these dividends to private investors.

- **By tapping into the growing sources of equity capital throughout the world, Metro Transport was able to reduce the amount of debt it had to issue to fund its capital programs. Equity is a form of "patient capital" that has been too long overlooked for public purpose capital facilities that are financed by governments or public authorities.**

Needless to say, the gut instinct of private investors who own equity shares in Metro Transport would be to press for policies that maximize its profits. To the public, this raised fears that Metro Transport would charge the highest toll rates possible while providing the least service it could get away with. So if this independent enterprise concept was to fly, it had to include credible protection of the public interest.

The usual way to accomplish this is through the traditional public utility model. Some sort of state government commission is created to regulate the enterprise's rate structure, impose minimum service standards, and generally ride herd on its operations through a host of micro-management oversight procedures that can generate lots of paper but too often compromise efficiency.

But the creators of Metro Transport came up with a better way.

- **This involved having a second group of owners for Metro Transport. These were the state government and the local governments in the metropolitan region, who transferred** ownership of their roadways to the enterprise. For which they received equity shares in lieu of cash, plus due representation on Metro Transport's board of directors.

- The gut instinct of these government owners was to push for policies that maximize votes for their elected officials. This generally translates into having Metro Transport provide lots of service while keeping toll rates as low as possible – the polar opposite of the natural agenda of the private investor owner group.

In theory, competition between the natural agendas of these two owner groups should lead to "balanced policies" for Metro Transport that mean reasonable service levels at toll rates that the public finds acceptable.

But as Arnold Rothstein and Johnny Torrio learned from contemplating the periodic blood baths that afflicted rival bootlegging gangs during the Prohibition era, competition can produce all kinds of disagreeable problems in practice. In the case of Metro Transport, these problems could take the form of policy stalemates that prevented a great many important things from getting done.

To avoid this, the creators of Metro Transport established a third group of owners.

- This group consisted of business firms whose sales revenues depended on the level of economic activity in the metropolitan region. They included commercial banks, utility companies, large retail chains, trucking and other business services firms, and media companies that lived off sales to local consumer advertisers.

- **The gut instinct of these owners was to push for Metro Transport policies to assure good, affordable transportation that's able to accommodate travel demand in a fiscally sound manner, so the region's economy (and therefore their sales revenues) can grow. This made them natural referees between the narrow profit maximizing agenda of the private investor group and the equally narrow "voter popularity" agenda of the government owner group. This greatly lessened the danger of policy stalemates.**

During the years since Metro Transport began operating, it delivered a host of improvements to roadway transportation that would have seemed like impossible dreams to motorists in the metropolitan region back in the early years of the 21st century. When revenues from penny-per-gallon motor vehicle fuel taxes had ceased to grow. When the over-programmed Federal Transportation Trust Fund ran short of tax revenues and had to renege on many of its promised construction grants. When appropriations for roadway maintenance from local government budgets had to give way to new spending for anti-terrorist protection, educational mandates, and other agendas with greater sex appeal. When the overall condition and capacity of the region's roadway system fell farther and farther behind what was needed to support the local economy.

Equally important, Metro Transport became recognized as the only practical source of new revenues to revitalize transportation in the region. This led to some interesting innovations.

One of them involved an ancient, virtually moribund railroad company whose right-of-way ran through the region from east to west and skirted the city's central business district (CBD). It had been in bankruptcy for many years and had long since ceased paying property taxes to any of the local governments along its right-of-way. But all this changed when the senior managers of Metro Transport put together an interesting deal.

- Under Metro Transport's leadership, the local governments that were owed many years of unpaid property taxes formed a Special Creditors' Committee and exercised their right to seize the railroad's right-of-way for non-payment of taxes. Which they immediately leased for a token sum to Metro Transport.

- Working closely with two large multi-modal goods-movement corporations that served the region, Metro Transport used some of the profits from its toll roads to upgrade the right-of-way's freight tracks and build a new rail/truck transfer facility in an abandoned railroad yard near the CBD. This enabled a significant number of goods movement trips to and from the region to be shifted from road to rail. Thereby reducing shipping costs to regional firms that depended on efficient goods movement services. And (not so incidentally) freeing up lane space for motorists.

- Metro Transport then turned around and formed a partnership with the region's bus-operating Transit Authority to build a light-rail line in the right-of-way. Metro Transport issued new debt (secured by its toll revenues) to supplement state government capital funds to fund this construction. This gave the region a modern rail transit line to shift some CBD-oriented commuting trips from automobile to rail. Freeing up still more lane space for motorists.

Some people were critical of the idea of using toll revenues provided by motorists to support these non-road transportation modes. But Metro Transport argued that the region (including its motorists) could only benefit from greater integration among what had too long been regarded as entirely separate travel modes. After all, every goods movement trip shifted from road to rail freed up roadway lane space for motorists. Ditto every CBD commuting trip shifted from car to light-rail, especially during high demand periods.

As Metro Transport's CEO stated in a public forum on the region's transportation needs:

> *"We've gotten into the bad habit of seeing transportation modes as a collection of kiddy rides in a public amusement park, where the popularity of each ride depends on its separate and distinct character."*

> *"But in the real world, transportation customers don't care about the physical distinctions between different modes. What they care about is moving themselves and their goods from door to door in the fastest, most efficient manner. If this means that a particular trip uses more than a single mode, so be it. And if integrating all modes into a single, seamless system of regional transportation requires using some revenues generated by one mode be used to help support another mode, who cares? It's the end result that counts."*

> *"This concept of cross-subsidization had long been practiced by some of the best managed multi-product corporations. What matters to them is the overall bottom line.*

If this can be boosted by having one product help support another within the larger corporate framework, then cross-subsidization is scarcely a dirty word. Why should it be any different in the transportation world?"

"That's why Metro Transport wasn't named "Metro Roadways." Our mission is to improve the region's **total** *transportation complex in an integrated manner. Because that's the best way to serve the public's mobility needs."*

Again, we should keep in mind that the true value of idealized models like Metro Transport don't depend on whether they can ever be implemented in the form they first appear. Rather, it lies in their ability to stretch our minds during the vision development process – by showing us some of the possibilities inherent in sound strategic visions.

This is how we harness essential feedback between vision and reality. Just as those who produced War Plan Orange did.

How to Develop Transportation Strategy

Most of us in the transportation community already have our own ideas about what an appropriate strategic vision should be like.

But our ideas aren't what matter. Rather, it's the ideas of our customers. And this is where things get really interesting.

More than a generation ago, management guru Peter Drucker stated that: "The primary goal of every enterprise should be to create customers."[1]

To make sure there was no confusion about this message, Drucker went on to tell us in no uncertain terms that the traditional accounting focus on generating profits is *not* a proper goal for any enterprise that wants to be successful. An adequate level of profits is simply one of the costs that the enterprise has to cover with its revenues – just like salaries and wages, payments to suppliers, and capital investments in new plant and equipment. Creating customers is the *only* goal that matters if an enterprise is to justify its existence in a modern capitalist society.

Drucker's revolutionary insights about the importance of creating customers became the driving force behind the management discipline we now call *marketing*.

Unfortunately, this choice of terminology is a poor one and has led to much confusion down through the years because an entirely different kind of activity has a prior claim to the name.

Remember when we were kids and heard our mothers talk about "doing the marketing"? This meant going to the supermarket to buy the weekly supplies of family groceries. To our mothers, marketing had nothing whatever to do with the task of creating customers for goods and services. It simply involved keeping the family larder stocked.

This may account for the confusion in many circles over what the management discipline called marketing is really all about.

But despite its ill-chosen name, the intelligent application of marketing as a management discipline has been the hallmark of every successful American enterprise during the last generation. And we must make it a cornerstone of our efforts to plan, build, and manage the kind of integrated transportation system that can properly support future economic growth. In short, responding to customer needs should be the primary driver for efficient allocation of transportation capacity.

The four most important components of marketing are:

- ***Defining who our customers really are.***

- ***Identifying important needs that these customers will pay good money to have satisfied.***

- ***Developing solutions that satisfy those needs.***

- ***Aligning the entire enterprise around creating value for customers.***

These are the most important tools for creating customers. And they're just as relevant for developing effective transportation systems as they are for developing effective computer software or automobiles or toothpaste.

So we should begin by *identifying important customer needs* in the arena of transportation. We may think we already know what these needs are. But our ideas are really just guesses because we have depressingly little factual information about what transportation customers themselves see their needs to be. And we can't expect to develop truly effective transportation by relying on mere guesswork.

We obtain this critical information about who our customers are and what they see their needs to be through a process known as market research.

Market research involves spending lots of face time with customers listening to them talk about their transportation needs. In this way, we gain a qualitative sense of how they define their transportation needs, which ones they regard as sufficiently important to be worth paying good money to have satisfied, what concerns they have about things like travel safety and security, and how they categorize themselves as transportation customers.

Listening to our customers will also help us identify the main issues we have to examine further through formal surveys. If these surveys are properly designed and statistically kosher, they'll provide us with the essential quantitative data needed to assess the relative importance of various transportation needs and to define priorities for meeting them.

The right kind of market research will give us, for the first time, the factual information we need to determine what an effective transportation system for the nation should look like to meet the needs of its many different kinds of customers.

But just as with analyzing the external environment for transportation, market research can't be thought of as a one-shot effort. Instead, it must be ongoing. For two important reasons:

The first reason is that the views of our customers are the only meaningful way we have to *measure our success* in developing the kind of transportation system that the nation needs. We have to let our customers tell us whether we're doing the right kind of job. This means listening to what they have to say at frequent intervals.

The second reason why market research must be ongoing is that *customer needs are likely to evolve over time*. Given the long lead-time needed to plan and build transportation facilities, we must try to get ahead of the curve in anticipating how customer needs are evolving. Simply playing catch-up ball is one of the reasons why so many of our major metropolitan regions are crippled by traffic congestion. Ongoing market research is the only way we can anticipate tomorrow's transportation needs soon enough to meet them in a timely fashion.

Planning and managing the ongoing functions of analyzing the external environment and conducting effective market research are major undertakings. But they must be done before we can develop a meaningful strategic vision of what transportation in America should look like. So we have to make some decisions about where the responsibility for carrying out these undertakings should lie.

The Responsibility Issue

In an ideal world, it might seem logical to assign this responsibility to the federal government's Department of Transportation (DOT). After all, we're talking about issues of national significance that the federal government should presumably handle.

But today's federal government is a far cry from the federal government of the 1930s and 40s. That government carried us bleeding and moaning out of the Great Depression. Developed and carried out the strategies to defeat Germany and Japan during World War II. Propelled us after the war into the greatest era of economic prosperity and world leadership we've ever known. And provided the national momentum that led to the Interstate Highway System, the Space Program, and ultimate victory in the Cold War.

The federal government of the 1930s and 40s seemed to epitomize the can-do spirit of American know-how like no other government in our history. And we could generally trust it to do things right. But today's federal government is a pale shadow by comparison. And we have little confidence that it can do anything right.

Fortunately, there are encouraging signs that state governments are willing to step into the vacuum left by a federal government that has lost too much credibility. Almost out of desperation, forward-thinking state transportation departments are already seeking out new ways to implement badly needed transportation improvements that don't rely on Washington. Even to the extent of forming partnerships with the private sector to tap its management expertise, marketing savvy, and capital sources.

This suggests that state transportation departments should assume responsibility for analyzing transportation's external environment and conducting market research among their customers. They might begin by tapping the resources of their state university systems.

Such an approach would build on the earlier tradition of states establishing colleges of agriculture to develop and promote new techniques for improving what was, for many of them at the time, their most important industry. Today's challenge may be to improve transportation rather than agriculture. But the challenges are similar.

Just as in agriculture, it's unlikely that all states will have the same mix of transportation demands. State DOTs are closer to their customers and instinctively more responsive to their needs once they have good information about what these needs are. At the same time, there's an encouraging trend among state governments to share information and ideas. The federal government can help by providing state DOTs with planning grant money to support ongoing programs analyzing the external environment and conducting market research.

Such a shift in responsibility and power from the federal government to the states isn't confined solely to transportation.

Rather, it's part of the much larger devolution issue that's attracted the attention of political economists like Gar Alperovitz, Alberto Alesina, and Enrico Spolaore. They've been exploring the question of whether the United States may have grown too large to be effectively managed from Washington any longer.

Way back in the early 1800s, James Madison thought this might become inevitable if the nation's population kept expanding. Economists like to call this phenomenon "*dis*economies of scale", though they shy away from using such academic gobbledygook in public.

Large-population "nation-states" like California and Texas are already moving in this go-it-alone direction. And not just in transportation. While smaller states like those in New England can band together in regional compacts to address common problems without waiting for Washington to bestir itself.

Since transportation is so intertwined in the national economy, there probably remains some role for the federal government to play (if only to justify its practice of taking the lion's share of every tax dollar that the economy generates). This could involve implementing as national standards new concepts that creative states have shown to work. Brokering agreements between neighboring states that share portions of vital intercity transportation corridors. Commissioning forward-thinking studies into the shape of the future, new transportation technology, better planning practices, etc.

Such a federal-state partnership could well be the future of a more democratic America. In which case, action on transportation problems could become one of the lead horses that truly workable forms of devolution ride.

Questions as Preludes to Answers

In the last analysis, this book probably raises more questions than it answers.

But that's how we learn. Because the process of developing strategy begins by asking the basic what and why questions in the right way. And to keep on asking them so their answers stay current with the escalating pace of change in today's world. There has to be a good fit between what an enterprise actually does and the demands placed on it by an external environment that's never static.

Only then can we proceed to develop meaningful strategic visions for what our transportation systems should look like. After which discussions of funding gaps and other issues concerning the tactical hows of translating these visions into reality start to make sense.

Admittedly, these tactical "how" questions concern the issues that we feel most comfortable discussing because they're closest to our experiences as transportation professionals. Also, because they seem most relevant to the pressures we're under to improve transportation. So we're naturally anxious to find out:

- ***What should we start doing?***
- ***What should we stop doing?***
- ***What should we keep doing?***

But the fastest way to come up with meaningful answers to these tactical questions is to frame them in the context of a truly effective strategic vision for the future shape of transportation in America. One that can be as successful as War Plan Orange was in guiding the U.S. to victory in the war against Japan. In this book, I've attempted to show some of the lines of thinking we should pursue to develop such a vision.

It seems apparent that we'll have to embrace some radical new beginnings to make all this work. Incremental changes to existing transportation policies and programs already rendered obsolete by history can't possibly get us far enough fast enough to meet 21st-century challenges. The laughing-stock scribblings in the 2005 Safe, Accountable, Flexible, and Efficient Transportation Equity Act: A Legacy for Users (SAFETEA-LU) surely demonstrate this. We need nothing short of a start-from-scratch revolution in how we develop and manage transportation if we expect to satisfy the growing mobility demands that are necessary for the nation's economy to grow.

Admittedly, this may be less than comforting to those transportation stakeholders who've grown fat and happy with the status quo. But they're kidding themselves if they think that turning a blind eye can insulate them from the consequences of the future. They'll simply wind up stranded on the beach. Like those unregenerate battleship admirals after Pearl Harbor who insisted that War Plan Orange shouldn't be adapted to incorporate the new reality of the aircraft carrier.

Note the liberal use of the term "We" throughout the book. And it's important to define this term properly.

In the narrowest sense, "We" means those who plan, design, finance, build, and operate transportation facilities and services. In other words, the people on the front lines.

But transportation stakeholders also include elected officials, managers, and technical professionals in Washington, state capitols, and local governments whose responsibilities involve transportation to one degree or another.

In the private sector, important stakeholders include the many firms that provide various kinds of services to move people and goods. Not to mention firms whose primary businesses involve selling goods and services to transportation providers in the public and private sectors.

Finally, the most important stakeholders of all are transportation customers. Whose concerns are too often overlooked.

In short, the collective "We" in transportation turns out to be much larger and more encompassing than many of us may have imagined. But it's vital that we hear all these voices if we're to develop a meaningful strategic vision of what American transportation systems should look like in the future.

Introduction: ANOTHER ANGLE

As Sol Grossman, a neighborhood Brooklyn bookmaker and Talmudic scholar, never tires of reminding his wagering customers:

> "The race may not always be to the swift, nor the battle to the strong. But that's still the way to bet."[2]

The street-smart wisdom that lurks behind this quip has more to teach us than may be immediately apparent.

After all, it's not absolutely positively guaranteed that we will end up reaping the bitter fruits of a national failure if we don't clean up our act when it comes to transportation. Isn't God supposed to have a long tradition of looking after drunks and lost children? So there's at least an outside chance that everything will still turn out fine if we continue to drift along in the same old way and never get around to coming to grips with our transportation problems.

Nor is it absolutely positively guaranteed that we will triumph over all adversities if we buckle down in a proper spirit of sack-cloth and ashes, make all the right decisions and investments, develop sound transportation improvement programs, and generally flagellate ourselves with upsetting changes in the way we've always done things. For if the odds are against us due to much larger reasons, we will still go down in flames. History is filled with stories of nations that lost their way in the world despite doing all the right things.

On the other hand, which makes more sense in terms of simple prudence? Keeping our fingers crossed as we whistle our way through the dark woods, or trying to understand how the clock ticks to make sure it tells the right time more than twice a day?

So let's look at transportation from another angle. One that's more down-and-dirty than we considered in the prelude, "Starting Over."

Many in the transportation community are warning that the nation is on a collision course with disaster. They say that our transportation infrastructure is in bad shape and getting worse, and incapable of meeting the demands of economic growth.

According to these folks, we're in no position to deal with such problems as:

- **The declining condition of the nation's transportation infrastructure.**
- **Its lack of capacity to meet the demands of economic growth.**
- **The growing inability of available funding resources to address these problems.**
- **Too much wasteful fragmentation among transportation modes.**
- **New homeland security needs and the escalating costs meeting them.**
- **Institutional impediments to "getting things done."**

Are these Cassandras right?

Well, let's look at the key questions that should be driving our search for a sound vision of surface transportation in America and how to make it real. *Driving Questions: Developing a National Surface Transportation Vision* outlines the current status of the nation's surface transportation system, what a long-range vision of the system might look like, and what we should do to turn this strategy into reality, and thereby transform our current transportation system into one that is once again the envy of the world.

The book focuses primarily on modes of surface transportation – roadways, railroads and rail and bus public-transportation systems – but also pays attention to the interconnections (or lack thereof) between these land-based modes and those that move passengers and goods by water and air.

We know from experience that transportation is just not on the radar screen for most business leaders or elected officials. They typically avoid hard decisions about how to rebuild the nation's surface transportation system, preferring instead to tweak what has effectively become a wasteful "pork-barrel" collection of projects that influential members of Congress use to build local voter support and campaign war chests.

For their part, the American public seem oblivious. Newspapers are fond of ranking the most congested cities in the nation, but generally the average American seems far more preoccupied with the mismanagement of offshore military adventures, internal security and terrorism, responses to natural disasters like Hurricane Katrina, and saving various entitlement programs from the budget axe. When it comes to transportation problems, they simply heave a sigh, suck it up, and leave for work a little earlier.

Transportation remains low on the public's priority list partly because the average citizen doesn't understand how the game is played. How is transportation actually funded? Who runs it and how? What impact does it have on our wallets? How does it affect our personal safety?

Perhaps such ignorance is only to be expected when the surface transportation agencies and industry keep telling us to make do with what we have, and then we should throw more money at the problems and extrapolate from what has worked in the past.

But as Albert Einstein once said:

"Today's problems cannot be solved by thinking the way we thought when we created them."[3]

Secretary of Transportation Mary Peters recently echoed this sentiment by noting the need to "find 21st-century solutions for 21st-century transportation challenges." Then she went on: "We can't assume that the methods of the past will work for the future. Instead, we are going to recognize that our transportation challenges have changed dramatically in the forty years since this department came into being, and so must our approaches."[4]

For better or worse, this is our reality, and it's wise we make the best of it. Thanks to changes in the domestic and global economies, the demographics of transportation users and new technologies, the needs of transportation consumers are constantly evolving. It's essential that the abilities of transportation facility and service providers keep pace.

Consider the Interstate Highway System, one of the most important parts of the nation's transportation complex. After 50 years of increasingly hard use and inadequate maintenance, it is fast approaching the end of its service life. Massive investments are needed to restore it to the functional and structural standards that would enable it to operate safely and efficiently, but current sources of funding are no longer sufficient.

For example, the Federal Transportation Trust Fund relies on revenues from the Federal Motor Vehicle Fuel Tax, but those revenues are running dry due to the rising costs of construction, fuel-efficient vehicles, and the increasing use of tax-exempt alternative fuels. And even addressing those federal fuel tax issues will hardly make a dent in the problem since much of the nation's surface transportation infrastructure is financed from other sources anyway.

As shown below, state and local governments already bear most of the costs of the nation's highway system, representing 79 percent of the $155 billion in revenues generated for the system in 2005. So dealing with safety, mobility, and obsolescence issues requires a joint effort from federal, state and local government, as well as transportation consumers and transportation providers in the public and private sector alike.

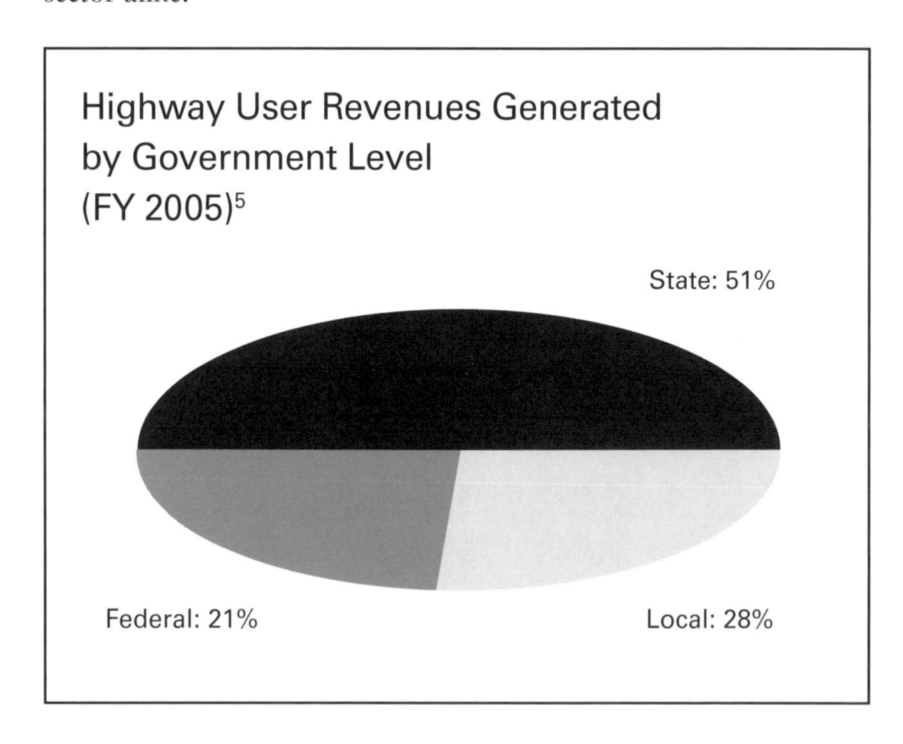

Most efforts to define the funding gap assume that past travel patterns will stay the same, and so very little thought is given to how such patterns will be affected by changes in domestic and global economies, domestic demographics, emerging technologies, and institutional arrangements. But the one thing we can be sure of is that the future will be different from the past.

Consider what the nation's surface transportation systems were like half a century ago. In those days:

- Most private carriers were highly regulated by the federal and state governments.
- Major competition occurred within modes, such as rail road and roadway, rather than between them.
- Toll-way development outpaced the improvement of the nation's non-tolled highway system (prior to authorization of the non-tolled Interstate System in 1956.)[6]
- The country's population was only three-fifths as large as it is today.
- The U.S. dominated the world's economic output and consumption.

And now 50 years later, the private carriers are largely deregulated, inter-modal competition is fierce while much of the highway system remains toll free, and the global economy has long since displaced the domestic economy as the U.S. has become a net importer of manufactured goods and a major consumer of foreign-produced goods.

Unfortunately, transportation revenues have not kept pace with replacement and expansion needs. As a result the system is clogged with more traffic. More users demand more mobility, accessibility, reliability and safety from a system barely able to function.

At least part of this is because the costs of developing and maintaining the nation's highway system have escalated faster than consumer price inflation. Federal and state governments contributed to the problem with a proliferation of mandates and regulations, by empowering groups opposed to highway construction, and by postponing maintenance that could have prevented premature reconstruction or replacement of highway links, thereby adding to the reconstruction backlog.

Another reason that the highway system is overextended is because the nation's rail system has shrunk since 1980 when the privately owned railroad companies were essentially deregulated. This led to a rash of line closures and trackage-rights agreements that allowed several railroad companies to use the same line owned by one of them. All of which diminished rail capacity and forced too many goods movement trips onto roads.

And so, without adequate fiscal resources, cost-effective business practices, safeguards for the public interest, and a sound vision of what transportation should look like, what the future holds is a declining quality of life for all Americans. The U.S. economy will fail to keep pace with the growth in the global economy while increasing congestion causes motorists to spend more potentially productive hours in idling automobiles and trucks along clogged arteries in the metropolitan areas that account for most of the nation's GDP.

The passage of SAFETEA-LU, signed into law August 10, 2005, left transportation stakeholders with little to celebrate. Guaranteeing funding for highways, highway safety, and public transportation totaling $244.1 billion over five years ending in 2009, the new legislation does little more than update previous reauthorization bills with modest additional funding, some new programs and more delegation of responsibility to state and local governments.

Meanwhile, as the victory champagne was rapidly going flat in Washington legislative offices, experts from both the public and private sectors warned that the highway portion of the Transportation Trust Fund would be unable to meet funding obligations beyond 2008, or 2009 at best. There is simply too little fuel tax revenue flowing into the fund to support the obligation levels built into SAFETEA-LU. The six-year reauthorization process for the half-century old federal highway program is no longer viable. Ditto the usual suggestions for reinvigorating the Transportation Trust Fund by simply increasing the outmoded Federal Motor Vehicle Fuel Tax. It's like the Biblical parable about putting new wine into old skins. It's bad for the wine, the skins and everyone goes thirsty.

And thus, if we're headed into a "perfect storm" – the eventual collapse of the nation's surface transportation program – there are three main factors accounting for it: declining transportation revenues; increasing costs of renewal, replacement, or expansion; and the growing dependency of individuals and businesses on automobiles and trucks. It doesn't help matters that the key stakeholders are not prepared to formulate a common strategy for the nation's future transportation system since many of them have conflicting interests.

For instance, while the public highway system and the privately owned freight railroad system are dependent on each other at such key loading points as ocean shipping ports and inland transfer yards, these modes compete with each other in moving goods. Similarly, the motor carrier and logistics industries that depend on the highway system traditionally oppose any increase in motor vehicle fuel taxes recommended by federal and state authorities. Who's supposed to pay? The tooth fairy?

Right now there is no agreement on how to address the current fiscal crisis looming over the surface transportation system, never mind the investments needed to meet future challenges, like:

- An increasing amount of foreign-made goods entering the country via ocean shipping ports and border crossings for trucks and trains.

- A growing number of active senior citizens.
- Improving coordination between transportation modes to leverage available public and private resources.
- Reducing the costs of the current program.

One of the thorniest decisions currently facing state governments is whether to award long-term leases of their existing toll roads to private-sector consortiums for large up-front cash payments. The real danger is the temptation for government to use these cash proceeds for non-transportation purposes like balancing operating budgets or funding new social welfare programs. Cannibalizing our largely debt-free highway systems by leasing high-volume segments to toll-charging private firms might seem nightmarish. But the temptation to do this can be irresistible as motor vehicle fuel taxes continue to lose their steam, as budget pressures grow, and as awareness blossoms of the latent toll revenue bonanza lying hidden in these roads. So the nation needs to develop an explicit, unified strategy that addresses the issue of private operation of highway corridors and networks.

Without a unified vision, we might be looking down the road at transportation programs and funding arrangements that may result in vast differences in design and service standards from state to state. This poses a threat to reliable and cost-effective transportation in corridors that cross state lines, leading to higher transportation costs, higher costs for consumer goods and a drop in the standard of living.

A Vision and Strategy for Transportation in America

My aim in *Driving Questions: Developing a National Surface Transportation Vision* is two-fold. First is to provide key decision-makers in the public and private sectors with a comprehensive perspective on the challenges facing surface transportation. Second, to identify the fundamental questions, the emerging opportunities and challenges, and the underlying principles that must be addressed before choosing tactics and technologies to transform the current system to meet the evolving needs of our citizens and businesses. Among other things, this means dispelling a host of myths and wrong-headed assumptions about how surface transportation is administered, funded, developed, operated, and maintained.

But first things first.

The essential purpose of transportation is to support economic activity by moving people and goods in an expeditious manner. So an effective strategy for surface transportation should emerge from a broad exploration of the various stakeholder needs now and in the future, and a realistic appraisal of what these stakeholders are willing to do to support a new and more effective surface transportation program. At the very least, such support will require more competition, more cooperation between modes of transportation, benefits-based funding, life-cycle cost control and making use of available capacity by exploiting emerging technologies.

Wait a minute. More competition and cooperation? Isn't this like recommending that sheep lie down with wolves?

Not if the experiences of private industry are any guide. It turns out that a great many corporations form joint ventures to pursue certain opportunities together, even when (like General Motors and Toyota) they compete tooth-and-nail in many markets. Why?

Because these corporations have learned that the escalating pace of change no longer gives them the luxury of gradually building up elaborate, vertically integrated structures of cross-the-board capabilities. One corporation may be a star player in product design and production. But its new product can be more successful more quickly if it can tap into another corporation's marketing savvy and extensive distribution network. And if that corporation lacks the time to enhance its product design and production capabilities, a joint venture for the new product makes sense. So the two corporations agree to link arms and go swimming together.

That's why Intel forms partnerships with hardware manufacturers to come up with new generations of personal computers that exploit each partner's skills in developing new technology while assuring glitch-free compatibility for PC users. Why Microsoft collaborates with independent software companies to develop new applications that can run on (and therefore enhance the value of) the latest version of the Windows operating system.

One of the great benefits of entrepreneurial capitalism is its ability to wash away the old stained-glass assumptions about how "our role is to make widgets." Today's successful businesses increasingly define their roles as "making money by creating new customers for better widgets." Under these circumstances, cooperation among different firms makes good economic sense. And so it can in the field of transportation.

Several key considerations for developing a new transportation strategy are:

- Transportation facilities and services must serve the needs of people and commerce in America in a cost-effective manner.

- The management of transportation should be customer driven, not bureaucracy driven.

- Government should promote the kind of market pricing that encourages transportation providers to become more customer oriented.

- Where appropriate, taxpayer funds should pay for capabilities that serve broad social purposes but whose costs cannot be funded through the market place.

- Adequate funding for surface transportation involves more than just additional revenues from traditional sources. Above all, it requires new revenue sources linked to the benefits transportation provides.

- Reducing the life-cycle costs of transportation facilities is a major priority. So is relying on greater competition to enhance the operational efficiency of facilities. Ditto using market pricing to ration travel demand where the supply of transportation capacity is limited.

- Increased competition among transportation modes and providers may result in some redundancies. But these are necessary to accommodate emergencies, breakdowns, and the seasonal demand of industries like tourism, agriculture, retail, and electric utilities.

- The purpose of linking transportation and land use is to capture the value of improved accessibility and mobility that transportation facilities provide. Therefore, capturing a reasonable share of this value is the most economically sensible way to fund transportation.

- Apart from direct pricing of transportation facility use, mechanisms for doing this include tax-increment financing, transportation-impact fees, transportation-improvement district assessments, and right-of-way donations.

- American freight carriers and shippers must become more active in promoting improvements and supporting prudent funding strategies, both reflecting the benefits they enjoy from improved accessibility and mobility.

These issues will help frame the key questions transportation policy-makers and decision-makers need to consider in developing a collective strategy for how we should meet our future mobility and accessibility requirements in an ever-changing environment of demographic, economic, technological, and political conditions at both the domestic and global levels. A flexible vision of where the U.S. is headed and where it should be headed is a prerequisite for developing the legislative, regulatory, funding and procedural changes to address the evolving needs of our surface transportation system.

Chapter 1:
Looking For Context

This chapter discusses both the external and internal factors that represent several major challenges facing surface transportation in America. These challenges can't be considered solely from an internal perspective. Transportation is closely linked to both domestic and international demands.

The two are intertwined and must be considered together in any effort to develop a meaningful vision for transportation beyond inadequate stopgap measures like SAFETEA-LU. Therefore, the context for the major challenges facing surface transportation in the United States is defined by the external and internal factors that it confronts.

External Factors

Sixty years ago, the U.S. emerged victorious from World War II and went on to dominate the world's economy for the next quarter century. In the late 1940s, the U.S. generated more than 90 percent of the world's GDP, a responsibility that was obviously not sustainable for long given the country's relative resources, demographics and socio-economic characteristics.

So over the last 60 years, the U.S. shared much of this burden with other developed and certain developing countries that could offer lower cost labor and governments willing to become more significant players in the global economy. American trade policies, international funding institutions, and multinational corporations have since spawned a global economy in which many nations around the world participate.

This policy-driven program made possible the post-World War II economic recovery of Germany and Japan, greater trade within our hemisphere with Canada and Mexico, and expanding trade with South Korea, India, and China. This trend will likely accelerate in the future with countries such as China, India, and even Vietnam emerging as major trading partners.

There may also be further efforts to consolidate the Western Hemisphere into a single economic block, free of trade barriers and currency restrictions, as the European Union (EU) consolidates its economic might with the addition of the Eastern European countries, Russia, and eventually England. In the future, Asian nations may follow suit and form their own bloc.

These global transitions will have profound effects on the United States' balance of payments and our ability to compete in certain markets as new competitors emerge to assume greater market share. America's greatest strengths lie in the stability of its political system, the size and diversity of its economic structure, and a high standard of living for a middle class that constitutes one of the greatest markets for foreign goods.

But despite our strengths, the concept of "Fortress America," a vital economy and society virtually impervious to external shocks, came to a crashing end with the 1973-74 oil crisis. This was the first of numerous efforts by the Organization of Petroleum Exporting Countries (OPEC) to flex its muscle and create an artificial shortage of crude oil. With these fuel shortages and subsequent high energy prices, it became clear that the fuel tax was not a reliable long-term source of revenues for the nation's surface transportation system.

Hence, like many other industries, the nation's transportation sector can no longer afford to believe it operates in a vacuum. But transportation's interconnectedness with other industries, nations and trade partners is also a source of opportunity.

Following then are several factors that will influence our nation's competitive position in the growing global economy and must therefore be taken into account when developing and implementing a comprehensive transportation vision for the next 20 to 30 years. This is not intended to be an exhaustive list, but rather the most significant external influences on the nation's transportation system.

Globalization of Trade

Despite its widely forecast demise throughout the better part of the last century, capitalism is alive and well and spreading across the globe. American corporations seek opportunities to export their goods while they import raw materials and finished goods, and open production facilities and service centers in developing countries where labor is much less costly.

Part of what's driving globalized trade is the creation of larger and more diversified corporations, both in the U.S. and abroad. While many large overseas corporations are supported directly or indirectly by their own governments, the end result is the same – a growing trend towards a global economy based largely on multinational corporations and international trade.

Global commerce has also been spurred with multinational corporations opting to base their production facilities in countries with lower costs for labor and raw materials, fewer environmental restrictions, and lower tax rates. These advantages have been especially appealing to corporations that manufacture clothes, shoes, and electronics. They have also attracted the telecommunications industry which has relocated call-in service centers to countries like India and the Philippines where English is widely spoken by an educated and relatively inexpensive labor force. Outsourcing has become more popular as large corporations have worked to reduce costs and become more competitive by becoming less vertically integrated.

Globalization moves in the other direction as well, when, for example, foreign automakers like Toyota and Honda open highly automated automobile and truck manufacturing plants in the United States to reduce the cost of shipping assembled cars and trucks overseas. And in cutting down on logistics costs by locating assembly plants closer to major metropolitan markets in right-to-work states with favorable transportation accessibility and local tax treatment, these foreign companies create jobs here in America.

Another factor is the growing globalization of both telecommunications and international travel, both for business and pleasure. These trends are expected to accelerate in the future, placing increasing demands on the transportation infrastructure that serves the movement of goods and people to and from the United States.

Changing Patterns of Trade

Total U.S. trade, (both imports and exports) has doubled since 1996, increasing from $1.3 billion to $2.6 billion.[7] Several major events over the past several decades have significantly influenced trading patterns both within the U.S. and globally.

The widespread adoption of standardized shipping containers has been the biggest breakthrough in encouraging the international integration of transportation modes.

As mentioned earlier, it began in 1956 when truck company owner Malcolm McLean launched the first shipment of goods containers between Port Newark, New Jersey and Houston, Texas. McLean recognized it was possible to increase productivity by eliminating the labor-intensive manual transfer of individual cartons of packaged manufactured goods between trucks and ships. Instead, he packed these cartons into standard-sized truck-trailer containers that could be moved by a crane between ships and trucks and carried by truck to and from dockside.

During the last 50 years, containerized shipping by water, rail, and truck has grown significantly. The capacity of container ships grew from 58 truck trailers up to 10,000 20-foot trailer-equivalent units (TEUs) for the largest contemporary container ships. As a result, the size of the standard container has grown significantly, from 20-foot to 40-foot and now to 53-foot, with an internal load capacity of 3,850 cubic feet. During the past five years alone, container movements grew by 69 percent, from 58 million TEUs in 2001 to 98 million in 2006. Containerized trade is projected to grow by another 37 percent during the next five years, to 134 million TEUs by 2011.[8]

Containerization has expedited the inter-modal flow of freight between water, rail, and roadways by significantly improving the productivity and reducing the cost of international shipping. And by moving imported containers across the country on double-stack, dedicated premium service trains, also referred to as the "land bridge."

In addition, the ability to lock and seal containers at their point of origin has meant enhanced security, a major issue in the aftermath of 9/11. Now efforts are underway to make containers even more secure with special detectors or scanners that can be linked to already existing GPS devices that facilitate tracking and documentation.

The Emergence of China as a major U.S. trading partner has led to a significant increase in international trade through Pacific Coast ports of Los Angeles and Long Beach and Seattle's Port of Sea Tac. This has been further stimulated by expanding trade with South Korea and Taiwan.

But container traffic volume at these ports has grown faster than dockside capacity connecting access facilities. This has led to major bottlenecks for moving goods from these West Coast ports across the largely unpopulated deserts and mountains to huge consumer markets in the American heartland. These delays have prompted many Asian shippers to reroute their ships around the southern tip of Africa to reach the larger array of East Coast ports with more ample container handling capability. Consequently, East Coast facilities like the vast Port of New York and New Jersey have begun to work with connecting railway systems to improve land-based port access routes by eliminating bottlenecks and expanding capacity on selected double-stack capable rail routes.

The Establishment of the European Union created a single trading bloc of 16 European nations with a common currency and no trade barriers that has became a major U.S. trade competitor. Western European nations were among Washington's most important trading partners, but now many EU members are conducting trade with each other instead.

The Collapse of the Soviet Union in the late 1980s and early 90s led to new opportunities for trade with Russia and Eastern Europe. But the EU has absorbed most of the potential for trade with these formerly Soviet-bloc nations, many of which are also seeking EU membership, which will consolidate the EU as a formidable trading bloc, at the expense of the United States.

The North American Free Trade Agreement (NAFTA) may herald a time when the entire Western Hemisphere from Canada to Argentina is a single trade bloc, perhaps with a single currency and tariff-free trade among all member countries. Canada and Mexico are already two of the U.S.'s largest trading partners, and as Latin American countries become more industrialized and politically stable, opportunities for trade between North and Latin American countries will increase. If so, it will call for road, rail, and waterway facilities, inter-modal capabilities integrating the two continents.

Thriving-or just surviving-in the Global Economy?

As the U.S. economy matures, it will become increasingly dominated by banking, insurance, health care, leisure and other service industries. At the same time, manufacturing will become more heavily focused on assembling products whose parts are largely produced overseas and are then sent to the U.S., Mexico, and Canada for final assembly and distribution to U.S. customers. These changes in the nature and patterns of goods moving to American markets will require significant upgrading and expansion of such inter-modal facilities as ocean shipping ports, bridges, tunnels, highway crossings, freight railroads, and airports.

Here are some key issues that could hinder our ability to thrive in the expanding global economy:

Cargo limitations at many of the nation's ports, due to inadequate waterside crane capacity and docking availability. Landside access capacity is limited because of truck congestion on feeder roads, lack of rail capacity, or height restrictions on double-stack rail cars. Furthermore, port service hours are restricted when local communities oppose nighttime operations.

Channel depth limitations at most U.S. ports limit deep-draft jumbo container ships' direct access. Such deep-draft ships must moor offshore and transfer their containers to shallow-draft barges or what are termed "lighters." This raises shipping costs, which imposes a disadvantage for U.S. ports that compete with deep-draft ports in Canada and Mexico for North American shipping business.

The Panama Canal is currently being expanded to accommodate larger vessels. This will increase the Canal's capacity and make it easier for Asian shippers to reach East Coast ports and avoid highly congested West Coast ports. There is also a proposal to build a new canal across Nicaragua that would be able to handle even larger ships than the expanded Panama Canal.

The existing U.S. surface transportation system was largely designed to handle domestic movements of people and goods within a self-contained economy. Inter-modal connectivity and capacity at the nation's major port and rail/truck terminals are suffering from limited investment. Without modernizing and expanding these facilities, the U.S. will begin to fall behind emerging nations that are investing heavily in transportation infrastructure. This is a major challenge to the economic vitality of the U.S. into the 21st century. It may even pose a greater threat to the nation than commuter congestion in and around our major metropolitan areas.

Internal Factors

The transportation industry accounts for about 11 percent (or over $1 trillion dollars annually) of the U.S.'s total gross domestic product. Its 20 million employees represent some 16 percent of the nation's total work force.[9] This giant industrial complex includes:

- The providers and operators of transportation systems and services.
- The industries that manufacture and maintain transportation vehicles, facilities and systems.
- The public employees who administer and operate government owned roadways, bridges, tunnels, and transit systems.

While the transportation sector is a key component of the nation's economy, it also serves a much larger role in supporting the rest of the nation's economic activity by providing essential mobility for people and goods.

Fifty years ago, the nation began developing a highly structured program of highway planning, funding, and development that produced one of the wonders of the modern world – the 46,800-mile Interstate Highway System. During the past 35 years, various changes to the federal-aid highway program have made it more sensitive to environmental, community, and multi-modal issues. There were also major changes in freight transportation and aviation during the 1970s and 80s, when the federal government deregulated the trucking, railroad, and airline industries to bolster more competition, operating efficiency, and customer service.

In recent years, the aging of the nation's transportation infrastructure coupled with the inability of traditional revenue sources to keep pace with surface transportation funding needs has spurred much debate about how to "fix the system." But certain key components of the internal environment must be considered as part of any strategy or vision to "fix the system" over the next 20 to 30 years.

Aging Transportation Infrastructure

Many in the transportation community claim that the most serious problem is the gap between the funds available to solve infrastructure issues and the revenues available to do it. They believe that more money will solve everything. But this assessment emphasizes the revenue side of the ledger and ignores the cost side. It reflects certain institutional shortcomings that need to be addressed.

Incentives to Defer Maintenance - As originally established by Congress, the Federal-Aid Highway funding program specified that Federal Transportation Trust Fund grants would cover up to 80 percent of the cost of new construction and subsequent reconstruction or replacement. There was no provision for ongoing roadway operations and maintenance, so these costs had to be borne entirely by state and local authorities.

Needless to say, state and local agencies realized it would be cheaper in the long run to cut back on spending for operations and maintenance and allow roadways to wear out more quickly, since the cost of reconstructing or replacing them would be largely covered by federal grants. The result was a dramatic example of the law of unintended consequences in its most virulent form.

State and local governments came to regard these mostly federally funded new highways as gifts from God. They under-funded annual highway maintenance, and used operating budget funds for other purposes. When highway links inevitably wore out before their time, state and local governments only had to worry about coming up with 20 percent of the total sum from their capital budgets since federal construction grants covered the rest.

What was all but forgotten in this dubious calculus were the economic costs incurred by motorists who had to struggle with increasingly decrepit highways, as well as plenty of congestion when highway lanes were closed for their phased restoration period – an inconvenience, as any driver knows, that always lasts much longer than advertised.

Although later reauthorization bills made federal funds available for rehabilitation, renewal, and reconstruction at levels comparable to new construction, the damage had already been done. The early years of the system saw little in the way of life-cycle asset management, and today the advanced deterioration of the nation's highway system is testament to the consequences of deferred maintenance and lack of preventive maintenance.

The price tag for restoration is astronomical, and at a time when a federal funding regime dependent on revenues from fuel taxes is least able to afford escalating construction costs. It goes without saying that the expanded capacity needed to accommodate the transportation demands of a growing economy and population is at this stage a moot point.

Misleading Public Sector Financial Statements - The accounting practices used in the American public sector have always given an incomplete picture of public infrastructure and as a result the American public has been misled about the true life-cycle costs of transportation facilities, schools and other public infrastructure. Most glaringly, capital assets have traditionally been written off as sunk costs in the years of construction with no provision for future reconstruction or replacement. No successful business firm could get away with such a practice.

Under standard private sector accounting regulations, a private firm that builds a new factory must include in its annual income statements a portion of its original investment in the factory as an operating cost (just like employee wages and payments to suppliers) before it can declare a profit. This cost is called depreciation. It represents the portion of the factory's asset value that the firm theoretically "uses up" each year to produce goods, and that it must therefore charge against its operating revenues.

In effect, the accounting allowance for depreciation generates a flow of cash that the firm can use to replace the factory's worn-out roof, electrical system, production machinery, and other infrastructure components. And if the firm funded the factory's original cost with borrowed funds, this means that the debt incurred is a one-time debt only. All subsequent expenses to repair or modernize the factory and its equipment are funded from the firm's depreciation allowances, no matter how many years the factory remains in operation.

But this sensible practice was ignored until recently by most state and local governments. Instead of recognizing depreciation as a current cost that must be covered by current revenues, the public sector has traditionally acted as though its infrastructure assets were again comparable to gifts from God (like raw land) that would never wear out.

Among other things, this means that when a state government issues bonds to build a new highway bridge, for instance, it takes on a debt that lasts forever. When that bridge wears out after years of heavy use, the state must issue new bonds to pay for its replacement since there is no accumulated reserve (depreciation cash) to fund this capital expense. The same thing happens when the replacement bridge wears out. And so on until the end of time.

Today virtually all state and local government borrowing power, federal grants and capital resources are needed just to fund the growing cost to replace or restore worn out capital facilities or pay interest on debt incurred to pay for these facilities. Nothing is left to fund construction of new facilities to meet rising demand.

Private think tank "goo-goos" (as legendary Robert Moses liked to call those who questioned his ability to part the metaphorical Red Sea) may scream that such practices delude the public into believing that they are paying the full cost of the public services they are entitled to, when they're actually passing along a large portion of these costs to their children and grandchildren by borrowing.

The glib response is that a certain amount of lying to the public is essential if American democracy is to function. A more thoughtful answer is that borrowing to fund a certain portion of public-sector operating costs makes good sense if it leads to a larger economy that we can pass on to our children (along with the debt that made this large economy possible, whose cost to them will have been deflated by inflation). But such philosophical considerations are outside the scope of this book.

Deferring Maintenance - The problems of aging and deteriorating transportation infrastructure also affect private transportation companies. Especially as they become increasingly subject to the competitive freedoms and pressures for greater efficiency brought about by deregulation in the airline, trucking, and railroad industries during the 1970s and 80s. While many of the productivity gains in the U.S.

economy can be traced to the pass-through effects of deregulation, they didn't come without certain costs that are only just now becoming apparent.

For example, a significant portion of funding needs for private transportation infrastructure are driven just by the need to catch up with deferred maintenance. The financial and competitive pressures leading up to and following deregulation forced some operators to keep costs down by, among other things, de-prioritizing maintenance. Freight railroad companies used their newly found competitive freedoms to under-invest in existing rail facilities and divest themselves of all but essential portions of their route system. Trucking companies deferred fleet maintenance to keep their rates competitive and await the results of ever-changing federal mandates specifying the type of fuel that must be used, fuel economy and emissions levels.

At the same time, old-line airlines defer fleet replacement as they struggled for survival due to burdensome union and pension obligations, the burden of extra security measures in the aftermath of 9/11, and an economic operating model that's right out of *Alice In Wonderland*. Airlines with aging fleets are especially burdened by the cost penalties of lower fuel economy among their planes, especially when fuel prices spike as they did during 2006.

Urban Highway and Transit Travel Growth

Travel volume has far outpaced the growth in surface transportation infrastructure for the past quarter century, largely due to economic variables and demographic changes.

The Influence of Economic Variables[10] - One of the most significant factors influencing transportation infrastructure capacity is the level of economic activity at the national level (as measured by the GDP) as well as at state, regional, or local levels and within different industries. Since economic activity generates demand for moving people and goods, the lack of sufficient capacity can constrain economic growth.

Some have argued that congested transportation facilities are a positive indicator of economic vitality, while relatively congestion-free facilities indicate unused capacity and reflect declining economic activity and the kind of out-migration we are seeing in many rural parts of the nation.

Here are some other economic variables influencing surface transportation system needs:

- **Inflation** is one of the factors that determine the level of interest rates and therefore the cost of capital. While domestic inflation rates are relatively low, inflation in the construction industry is much higher due to massive infrastructure build-ups in China and India that boost market prices for such construction commodities as steel, concrete, and asphalt. As a result, many domestic highway construction programs in the U.S. are facing increases of 20 to 40 percent. This is causing these programs to curtail the number of projects that can proceed.

- **Employment Levels** can be measured either in gross terms or as percentages of the total labor force. Either way, high employment levels indicate a robust economy and consequently demand greater capacity to move people and goods, especially by highway.

- **Capital Formation** by the private and public sectors. Potentially, capital formation in various insurance and pension funds can be tapped to generate new capital funds for highway and transit projects. But realizing this potential requires a realistic expectation of acceptable rates of return to private investors from roadway tolls, annual service payments by government, or economic development fees. If this requirement can be met, the private sector can become a significant new source of capital for transportation projects.

  Private investors have already expressed interest in U.S. highways that can be tolled and might be available for long-term leases in return for the cash flow from rising toll schedules. Indeed, the Chicago Skyway, the Indiana Toll Road and the Pocahontas Parkway in Virginia were leased on a long-term basis to a consortium of private firms from Spain and Australia.

- **Government Fiscal Picture:** The fiscal condition of the federal, state, and local governments constitutes another set of economic factors that could affect the ability of government agencies to fund surface transportation projects involving reconstruction, replacement, or expansion. This is especially important where state and local governments are prohibited from using debt financing or running budget deficits.

Demographic Changes

Ultimately, it is people who produce GDP, demand transportation of various kinds and in various quantities for various travel purposes, and generate the financial resources to fund transportation systems.

Key demographic factors that will significantly influence the future requirements for surface transportation include:[11]

- How many people will live in the United States at various points in the future.

- The locations where they are likely to live (by state, by local region within each state, and by multi-state regions like the East and West Coasts). The largest growth in population over the next 30 years is expected in the South (55 percent) and West (33 percent), with the Northeast and Midwest growing only by 12 percent.[12]

- The proportion and number of single-person versus multi-person households, with and without children. This has a significant impact on housing location choices between urban areas (favored by single persons or couples without children) and suburban areas (favored by couples with children).

- The proportion of the population by age group. The aging of the baby-boomer generation means that a growing proportion of senior citizens with increased political clout will demand new mobility services that have never been confronted in the past.

- The size of individual or family incomes, which helps to determine how much individuals can pay for transportation and housing, which are typically trade-offs between each other (the longer the commute the less expensive the residence).

- The level of education, with more highly educated people being more discerning about what they will pay for in the way of new technology and more willing to make use of these devices.

Summary

The external environment, especially in taking advantage of the changing patterns of trade, represents an opportunity for transportation to support and enhance our economic power. So, we need to address some of the issues limiting our ability to participate in the expanding global economy.

And yet it is in the internal environment where resistance to changing or "fixing the system" comes from the institutional framework of the public and private sectors who have long dominated the surface transportation program, especially the highway system.

The effects these external and internal factors have on our current and future programs and systems are the subject of the next chapter.

Chapter 2: Searching for Meaning

In seeking to develop a new vision for surface transportation in America, it is important to understand the consequences of the external and internal factors confronting the U.S. economy, its citizens, and its surface transportation system, both now and into the future. This chapter draws on the previous chapter to explore the implications of these factors for our nation's mobility, quality of life, economic vitality, and competitiveness.

Changing Mobility Requirements

Research from Europe suggests that the most significant factors contributing to highway use and the need for added highway capacity are growth in population and the GDP, as well as rising GDP per capita, which occurs when the growth in economic output outpaces the growth in population.[13]

Ever-Expanding Mobility Needs

Growing transportation congestion can in part be attributed to the rapid growth of both the U.S. population and its service-based economy coupled with much slower growth in surface transportation capacity. In late October 2006, the U.S. population reached the 300 million mark. It took only 39 years to reach this milestone after passing the 200 million mark in 1969. According to the U.S. Census Bureau, the nation's population is expected to reach the 400 million mark around 2040, in just 34 years. In short, the nation's population is on track to double in only 73 years, the course of a single lifetime.

Americans are living longer productive lives. Rising immigration is adding to the proportion of foreign-born residents. Life-style choices are becoming more diverse. And housing location choices are expected to continue to favor suburban living in the Southeast and Far West. The result will be a greater diversity of citizens demanding more transportation choices, capacity, and capabilities. This is equally true of businesses that serve the needs of the nation's residents.

These demands pose a double challenge for transportation agencies and firms. During the 1970s, public funding for surface transportation infrastructure and services increased. At the same time, deregulation of commercial airlines, motor carriers, and railroads increased productivity, which enabled them to keep pace with transportation demand into the 1980s. But since the beginning of the 90s, transportation system growth has lagged behind increases in demand for moving people and goods. The result is increasing congestion, especially within major metropolitan regions and in intercity corridors of the national highway system.

Changing Nature of Mobility Needs

Demographic changes will also impact decisions about where goods and services are produced and where they are consumed due to sharp differences in the respective economic contributions of different age groups. For example, those over 65 generally demand fewer goods and more services. What they require from the transportation system is different from what families with school-age children do. Thus the changing demography of the U.S. will create a constantly changing transportation topology.

Policy decisions concerning immigration levels and the treatment of unregistered aliens may also impact transportation needs across the nation. For example, less immigration and a significant reduction in the number of unregistered aliens may alter the transportation needs of citizens, both in terms of goods movements and individual travel patterns.

Since the average age of immigrants tends to be lower than the average age of native-born Americans, the nation's average age will rise if policy decisions result in immigrants accounting for a smaller number of U.S. residents. Consequently, there will be a larger percentage of senior citizens than is currently projected, and thus relatively less demand for goods and more demand for services.

Unless the accessibility and mobility demanded by a diverse citizenry and economy are accommodated, these demographic projections forecast a future scenario with more traffic congestion and less productivity. The issues that need to be addressed then are:

- Funding and provision of transportation infrastructure.
- Land-use patterns involving housing and commercial space for offices and retail stores.
- Changing forms of land use and the transportation services to serve them.
- Applying technology to more efficiently use available

transportation capacity, control congestion, and provide additional funds by charging consumers directly for use.

Highway Congestion

Traffic congestion is widely regarded as one of the greatest challenges facing motorists and highway operators in metropolitan regions across the country and highway operators within metropolitan regions. It is estimated that congestion costs the U.S. economy $168 billion a year, a number that's grown by an average of 8 percent per year since 1982, more than twice as fast as the economy during the same time.[14]

Congestion slows traffic, increases air pollution and increases the potential for accidents, and reduces effective highway capacity as more vehicles attempt to use the roadway. Beyond a certain volume of traffic per hour per lane, adding more vehicles reduces the bumper space between vehicles. This causes drivers to slow down, thereby reducing the average speed of traffic. Lower speeds mean fewer vehicles passing a given point per hour.

From 1980 to 2002, the number of miles traveled grew by 90 percent, while the number of lane-miles of highways increased by only 2 percent.[15] In effect, metropolitan areas have been consuming their highway capacity with the result that highway speeds have sharply declined and any given highway's effective capacity during periods of maximum demand is far below its design capacity. The practical effect is like taking highway lanes out of service.

Unlike access to, for example, seats in movie theaters, most of the nation's highway system is available to motorists without direct charge. The perception is that highway lanes are "free goods," like public parks. But of course they are not free, and now the capital funds are increasingly consumed by efforts to rehabilitate, reconstruct, or replace aging highways built 40 to 50 years ago and nearing the end of their effective service lives. Consequently, fewer dollars are available to boost capacity by building new highways or adding lanes to existing highways.

Continued growth in population and economic activity, expansion of suburban boundaries, and the increasingly mobility-intensive lifestyles of the population will only add to the congestion woes of highway users, especially commuters and truckers who often do not have a choice of when to travel. One quick-fix solution from the 1980s and 90s, carpooling, which was designed to boost the person-carrying capacity of highways, failed when motorists insisted on retaining the flexibility, comfort, and convenience of driving alone. That's an instructive reminder that quick fixes won't solve the very real issues.

Let us consider our options:

- Accept the fact that traffic congestion is an inevitable consequence of population growth and economic prosperity. Prepare to put up with more time wasted in traffic jams, higher prices for the goods we consume as the cost of moving them to market escalates, and worsening air pollution as more motor vehicles spend more time making trips and at low speeds that magnify their polluting impact.

- Reduce the level of economic activity in major metropolitan regions so the travel demand it generates is modest enough to be accommodated at free-flowing traffic speeds on existing highways. But since the top 20 metro regions produce most of the nation's economic activity, this means placing American society on a diet of lower living standards – for everyone except the very rich.

- Reallocate a significant portion of the economic activity in these regions to nighttime hours when most highway capacity is unused rather than continuing to cram it into the standard daylight hours. This would involve some fairly heroic social engineering. In extreme cases, it could mean converting some of these urban areas into 24-hour societies like Gary, Indiana was back in the days when its steel mills operated around the clock.

- Gradually rebuild these metro regions into high-density urban environments like Hong Kong, where public transportation accounts for more than 80 percent of all daily commutes, and automobile ownership is limited to only 16 percent of the population. The same could happen here, given the right central planning, where most commuter traffic would be accommodated by subways, commuter rail, light rail, and express buses running on dedicated highway lanes. This would leave metro-area highways relatively free to offer to trucks and other commercial vehicles much shorter trip times.

- Build our way out of congestion by adding new lanes to existing highways. Then use differential highway pricing to induce motorists to make lower priority trips during lower demand periods or on less popular roadways. Given the relatively flat curve for the price elasticity of highway demand, pricing is likely to produce enough revenue to make highway expansion self-financing. Also, there should be enough left over to fund ongoing maintenance for the entire roadway system to assure that it can face each morning's travel demand in something like showroom condition.

In the abstract, all five of these options seem logical enough, but we're in the real world of 21st-century America where only the first and last choices are really plausible – either suck it up and learn to live with congestion or build and bill. As for the first, the fact is that much of the general public and their elected officials appear to have surrendered to the notion that congestion is inevitable and have come to accept it as an unavoidable consequence of population growth, economic activity and individual travel.[16] The problem is, however, that by choosing the default option, we're locking ourselves in and limiting our ability to move and the economy's potential to grow.

Environmental Considerations

The National Environmental Protection Act of 1970 (NEPA) already imposes significant cost and schedule constraints on the planning and development of surface transportation infrastructure. Federal surface transportation laws and regulations have interpreted NEPA requirements as mandating various levels of detailed analysis to determine the environmental impacts of proposed facilities or services, alternative courses of action, and different ways to mitigate any negative impacts. In effect, the federal government has interpreted the Clear Air Act and its amendments as prohibiting new highway facilities that increase capacity in those metropolitan areas that have not attained federal air-quality standards with few exceptions. Therefore, the local Metropolitan Planning Organization (MPO), the authority responsible for approving each metropolitan area's Transportation Improvement Plan (TIP), cannot include projects that are likely to increase highway traffic in non-attainment areas.

Innovative Approaches

During the next 30 years it is unclear how environmental issues will influence the type and use of surface transportation facilities and services, either through further regulation or the development and introduction of new technological developments. Growing concerns over global warming and local efforts to adopt the air quality objectives of the Kyoto Agreements (which the U.S. government has not signed) might further impede efforts to add new roadway lanes.

However, proposed solutions to these environmental issues tend to favor strategies aimed at increasing the use of public transit, car pools, and van pools. These strategies are more likely to be blessed by many environmental groups when a new highway includes special lanes that accommodate high-occupancy vehicles (HOVs) at little or no cost while charging high fees for drive-only vehicles. In effect, this means we can build new highway lanes that charge tolls so long as we waive tolls for buses, passenger vans and car pools.

Examples include lanes originally designed only for HOV use in the peak travel direction (HOV lanes) but subsequently converted to high-occupancy and tolled single occupancy lanes or high occupancy tolled (HOT) lanes. Also, building new lanes parallel to existing highways and tolling them for all users (express lanes). Plus new construction of express tolled lanes where free access is provided only to vehicles with very high occupancy (vans and buses carrying at least nine people), which are called Super-HOT lanes.

An example of the latter is the upgrading of California's I-15 express lanes north of San Diego to Super-HOT lanes by adding capacity designed to accommodate Bus Rapid Transit (BRT), which can provide express transit service without the need for high-cost fixed-rail guide-ways. These Super-HOT lanes have special slip ramps serving park-and-ride lots built for patrons of the BRT services. Under this arrangement, high occupancy vehicles are guaranteed a swift and reliable trip downtown on lanes where single occupancy vehicles (SOVs) are charged a variable toll that increases with the level of congestion on the special lanes.

Environmental and transit advocates favor these approaches because of their potential to influence driver behavior and modal choice, reduce congestion and emission levels, and provide toll revenues to help offset some of the costs of the new alignment and BRT ramps and parking facilities. Transportation planners also cite the costs saved in not having to build more lanes to accommodate the same number of travelers in the corridor.

These complementary results are accomplished by:

- Increasing the overall vehicle-occupancy rate throughout the corridor.

- Increasing operational efficiency within the corridor through congestion-based differential pricing.

- Reducing stop-and-go driving and traffic-halting incidents, which cause engine idling and increased emissions.

- Instituting real-time traffic management using Intelligent Transportation Systems (ITS) technology such as:

– Automated vehicle classification and tolling equipment.
– Real-time displays of travel time and variable SOV toll rates.
– Corridor monitoring cameras to facilitate traffic management and real-time incident response.
– Variable message signs to alert drivers to incidents and alternative routes.

Currently there are 62 congestion-reducing project initiatives operating, under development, or receiving funding under the Value Pricing Pilot Project (VPPP) program administered by the Federal Highway Administration (FHWA).[17] Many of these projects involve HOT lane conversions of HOV lanes, express lanes, and variable pricing of tolled and other priced lanes. These projects are primarily aimed at relieving congestion and managing travel demand.

The number of VPPP projects are listed below by type:

- Priced New Lanes - 18
- Variable Pricing On Toll Facilities - 14
- Regional Pricing Initiatives - 10
- Converting HOV Lanes To HOT Lanes – 8
- Usage-based Vehicle Charges - 6
- "Cash-Out" Strategies/Parking Pricing - 3
- Cordon Tolls - 2
- Fair Lanes - 1
- Truck Only Toll Facilities – 1

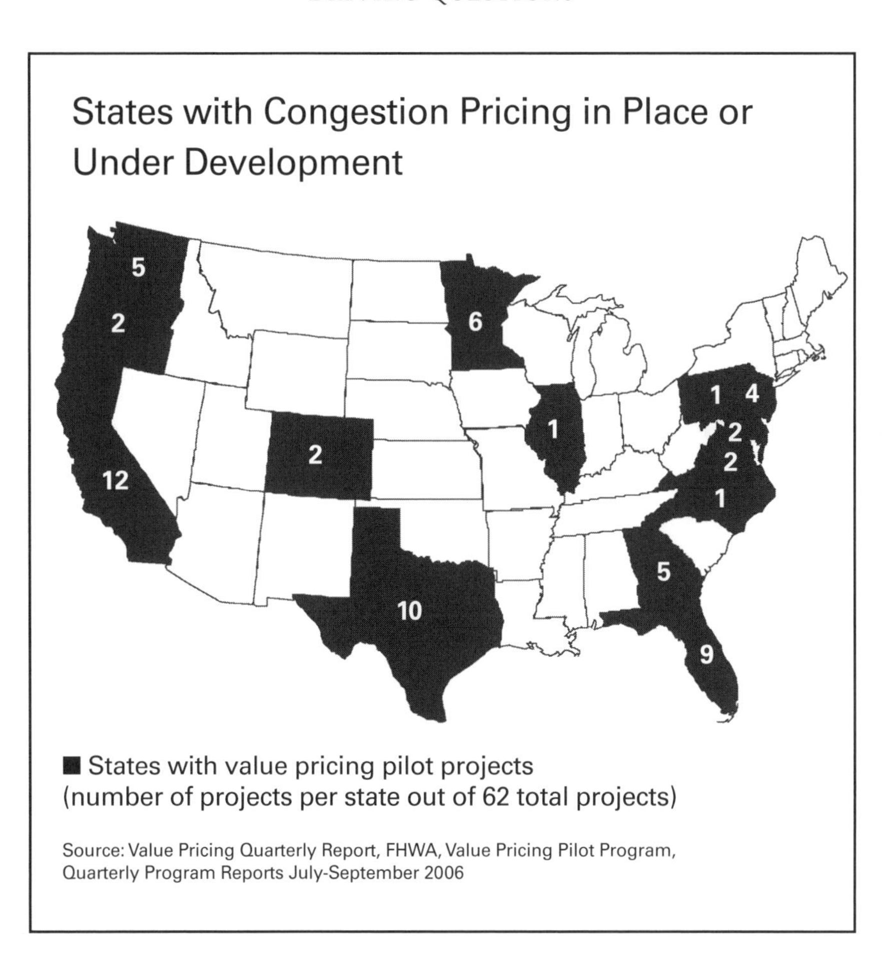

Equity and Direct User Charges

An important consideration in adopting congestion pricing is the notion of equity between those who suffer the consequences of congestion (delays, crashes, poor fuel economy, air pollution, and road rage) and those who choose to pay for the congestion-free alternative.

In the main, this is analogous to a senior citizen living on Social Security who can't afford to go to the movies on Saturday nights because of high ticket prices during high-demand hours and other moviegoers who are rich enough not to care what they spend. And yet the retired senior citizen has the option of going to the movies on weekday afternoons when ticket prices are much lower and the richer moviegoer is at work.

The difference, however, is that going to the movies is a discretionary activity while travel is usually non-discretionary.

Under the current price-free roadway arrangement, all motorists regardless of their incomes suffer the consequences of congestion whether they choose to or have to travel during peak time. This is a variation of how the Soviet Union and other Soviet-bloc nations rationed their chronic shortages of consumer goods. Prices were set low enough for everyone to afford. But you had to spend lots of time waiting in long lines to buy anything.

Capitalist America has long since accepted the logic of having to pay for scarce goods, and congestion pricing simply extends this concept to travel on limited-access highways. It offers motorists the choice of paying a certain number of dollars for faster travel on congestion-free toll-highways for high-priority trips (like going to work), or paying in increased travel time for zero-dollar travel on toll-free roadways for lower-priority trips.

Under the current arrangement, there is no choice and the customer is at the mercy of the poorly operated system. As for lower-income motorists who might not be able to afford to pay for congestion-free toll highways to get to work on time, they would be entitled to the same sort of discounts that public transit systems are required to offer elderly and disabled passengers.

Ultimately, a big part of the answer to roadway congestion is to use pricing to influence driver choices in ways that reduce peak period demand (while, not so incidentally, providing new financial resources to build more transportation capacity). Multi-modal alliances between highway and transit operators are a way to leverage both approaches (as in the BRT-on-HOT-lane scenario described earlier). In this case, a good solution is possible for all stakeholders. Travelers making high priority trips have the option of paying for faster trips, or paying nothing to make their low priority trips on congested roadways.

In the future, the introduction of non-polluting propulsion systems for automobiles could eventually eliminate the basis for prohibiting the addition of highway capacity in metropolitan areas that don't meet federal air-quality standards and greatly simplify the environmental review of highway infrastructure development. But such alternative propulsion systems would further diminish motor vehicle fuel taxes as a viable source of funding for the highway and transit programs. Offsetting this revenue loss would require the development and implementation of alternative sources of funding tied to vehicle use, BTU consumption, or vehicle prices. These are all important considerations in developing a vision for transportation in America during the first half of the 21st century.

Escalating Construction Costs

The cost of developing highway infrastructure has skyrocketed over the years, growing much faster than available capital funds at double-digit annual rates on such materials as steel, asphalt, concrete, and aggregate. This is attributed to a number of factors, including:

- The ability of environmental and community advocacy groups to impede and litigate against projects without reference to their need and social benefits.

- Higher project planning costs because of the need to accommodate numerous policy considerations and special interest groups.

- Federal promotion of failed initiatives such as High-Occupancy Vehicle Lanes and various Intelligent Transportation System (ITS) concepts that lack user demand or appeal.

- The increasing amounts of steel, concrete, and asphalt that China and India now consume, which drives up the prices for U.S. transportation infrastructure development.

- Loss of available transportation facility corridors as the freight railroads continue to shrink their networks by abandoning existing rail lines that could be reserved for future highway or public transportation uses.

In other words, the federal surface transportation program has stimulated the increase in transportation infrastructure costs even while it constrains the sources of funding for developing, expanding, or rehabilitating these facilities.

Lack of Operating Management

For many years, state and local highway agencies planned and built highways and roads, leaving operational responsibility to motorists. Their behavior was regulated by fixed traffic control devices defined by the Manual of Traffic Control Devices (MUTCD) and enforced by state and local enforcement authorities.

In the early 1990s, the federally sponsored Intelligent Transportation Systems program sought to improve the efficiency and safety of roadway facilities with new technologies. One useful application was Variable Message Signs, used to warn drivers of road closures, crash locations, congestion areas, and alternative routings. Other ITS initiatives included short-range radio transmission of traveler information, and a dedicated phone number for traveler information (511). However, over the past 15 years, most applications have seen mixed results, largely because ITS technology manufacturers pushed their products on the traveling public without considering consumer interest in the products provided.

Without doubt the most successful ITS initiative was electronic toll collection (ETC), which collects tolls without forcing motorists to slow down or stop. In its most sophisticated application, ETC has replaced the old-fashioned tollbooth with an overhead gantry that supports short-range communication with on-board vehicle transponders. This technology automatically deducts the toll from the motorist's pre-paid account. Photo-recognition equipment records the license plates of those vehicles without transponders so their owners can be billed later, typically with a small penalty in the form of an administrative fee to encourage future transponder use.

In recent years, auto manufacturers have made great use of ITS technology, many are already features of luxury vehicles produced by Lexus, Infinity, BMW, Mercedes Benz, and Cadillac, like in-vehicle navigation assist systems; traveler assist communication systems (such as GMC's OnStar and Mercedes Benz's TeleAid); anti-lock braking systems (ABS); automatic cruise control, rear-view camera assist when backing up; on-board diagnostic sensors; and voice-activated features such as driver instructions, audio controls, and cell phone use.[18]

Since the automobile manufacturing industry has a better grasp of what kind of advanced technology consumers want and for what purposes, the development and deployment of ITS technology is likely to continue to come from the vehicle manufacturing industry rather than the road-building industry.

Focus on Moving People and Goods

The traditional concern of state and local transportation agencies has been about generating roadway lane-miles and the vehicle-miles-of travel that these lanes serve. There has been too little attention given to customer service and improving the use of available transportation infrastructure. In part, this is because there is no meaningful pricing for available highway capacity. Whenever a valuable resource like highway lanes is not priced, it becomes overused to the point of diminished access, shortage of available capacity, inefficient congestion that lowers the effective capacity of highways as more and more motorists use them, only to find their travel times increasing and trip reliability decreasing.

This is especially critical for commercial vehicle operators and the shippers they serve. The rising popularity of just-in-time delivery service that minimizes warehousing costs demands fast travel and highly reliable trip times. When congestion interferes with these requirements, truck-dependent manufacturers may have to eat the costs of slowing down their assembly lines because of parts shortages. Trucking firms also suffer as their profit margins are worn away by the extra costs of drivers spending more time on the road.

For the railways, the pressure to reduce its maintenance costs has led the rail freight industry to abandon a lot of the track capacity that existed before rail deregulation in 1980. This reduces rail's ability to serve shippers who need timely and reliable freight deliveries. All too often, they're forced to use trucks instead. But rising truck volumes further congest highways in the largest metropolitan regions, which generate most of the nation's GDP.

Each of these factors has made transportation less reliable while increasing the time and cost of moving people and goods. Their collective impact is especially severe in urban areas and around inter-modal transfer points that serve the nation's major seaports. The result is the pervasive decline in the ability of the nation's economy to grow fast enough to meet its burgeoning social needs.

Funding Shortfalls

The fiscal challenges facing public transportation agencies and private transportation providers are a consequence of decreasing growth in revenues combined with the increasing costs of building and operating transportation facilities. As shown on page 88, projections show that the Highway Trust Fund account balance will fall below zero by 2009, with available Trust Fund balances projected to drop from one-third of Federal-Aid Highway Obligation Limitations in 2004 to a deficit of 5.6 percent by 2009.[19]

There are various well-documented reasons for this set of circumstances: There is the declining growth in revenue from the motor vehicle fuel taxes that support the Transportation Trust Fund; competitive pressures among private-sector freight-carriers that constrain revenues; and the escalating costs of materials used to produce transportation facilities and equipment.

It is this "perfect storm" – increasing demand for transportation, declining revenue growth, and the escalating costs of construction –

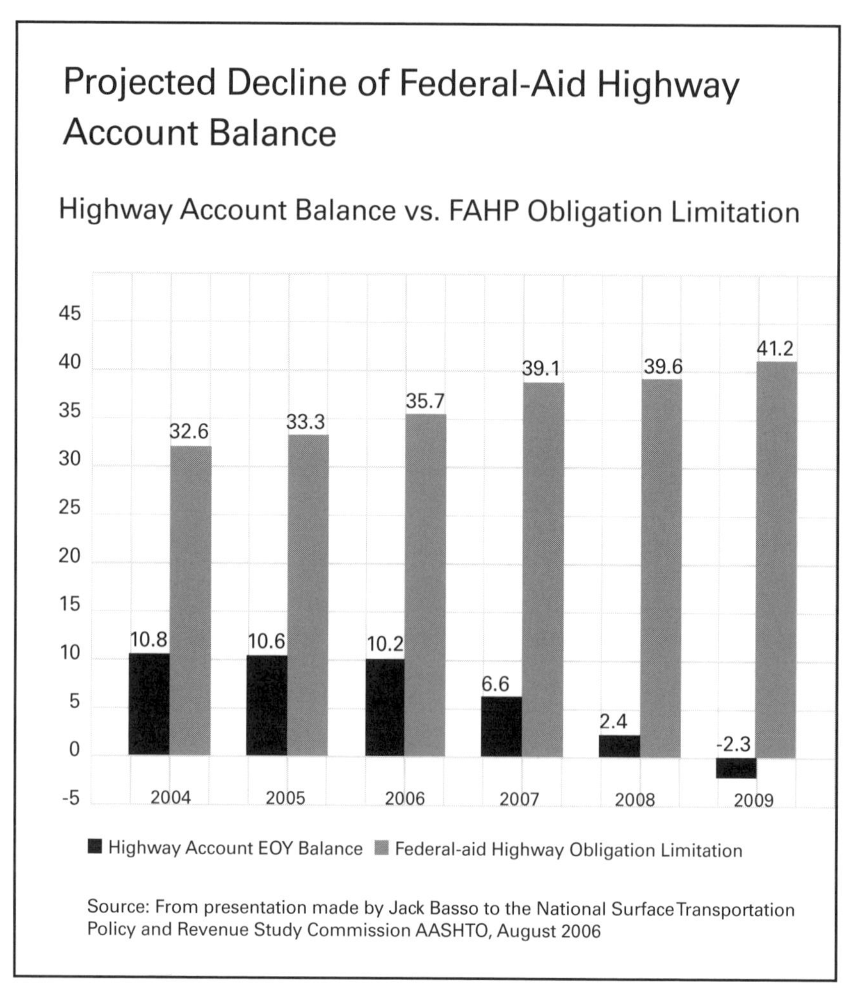

that is forcing public- and private-sector stakeholders to rethink methods of planning, funding, development, delivery, operation, and management of the nation's surface transportation assets.

Growing Gap between Costs and Revenues

It is estimated that up to $5.3 trillion will be required during the first quarter of the 21st century just to restore the nation's existing highway and transit systems to a state of good repair and to keep pace with growing travel demand. After allowing for federal, state and local funding, one-third of this amount remains unfunded.[20]

Much of the blame for the funding crisis is due to the reluctance of elected federal and state officials to increase the fuel tax, which the program depends on for much of its funding. The revenues are decreasing thanks to improved vehicle-fuel efficiency, the development of substitute energy sources, and the use of tax-exempt fuels like ethanol.

As taxes, rather than market-based pricing, these revenues are vulnerable to the attrition of purchasing power as transportation program costs increase and tax rates remain unchanged, and they will be increasingly unable to provide the necessary financial resources to support the highway program. The chart on page 90 indicates the decreasing purchasing power of the federal fuel tax, falling by one-third over the seventeen-year period to end in 2010.

It's worth noting that these projections assume, first, that the nature and use of the highway system will continue to follow past patterns and second, that the entire system needs to be restored to a state of good repair as soon as possible. In reality, transportation systems are not normally maintained at a uniform level of service or condition due to the cyclical nature of facility use and deterioration. Early projections typically overestimated capital requirements, often by a factor of 200 percent because it was mistakenly believed that the system had to be brought up to good-to-excellent condition all at once, rather than in cycles.

The overestimates also tried to anticipate and accommodate the inevitable cuts made by state legislative committees as well as the political pressures encouraging more projects to be included in capital improvement plans than could ever be fully funded. This resulted in project backlogs whose total costs were many times the funding capabilities of the sponsoring agencies.

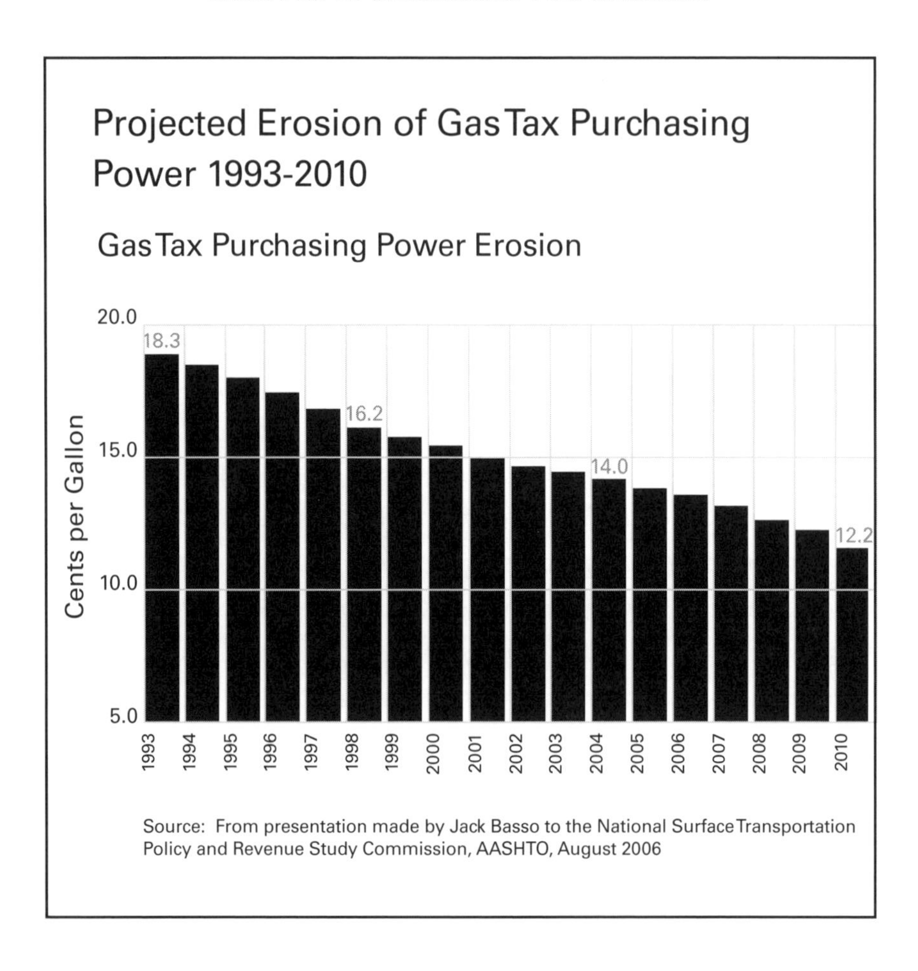

Source: From presentation made by Jack Basso to the National Surface Transportation Policy and Revenue Study Commission, AASHTO, August 2006

Growing Gap between Transit Costs and Revenues

The problem of project requests swamping available funding also affects the transit program. With earlier investments in major new rail systems in San Francisco, Washington, Baltimore, Atlanta, and Miami in the 1970s, plus construction of light-rail lines in cities such as Baltimore, Buffalo, Dallas, Denver, Houston, Los Angeles, Portland, Sacramento, St. Louis, San Diego, and San Jose during the past 30 years, some of these same cities are requesting additional funding to expand their systems. Still others are proposing additional fixed-rail guide-way systems.

Since 2000, there have been 39 New Starts projects approved by FTA, 15 of which are extensions of existing heavy- and light-rail projects. Another 13 are new light-rail projects, 4 are new commuter rail projects, and the remaining are for capacity improvement (1), reconstruction (2), and airport access projects (3). Only one of these New Starts Projects is a bus project.[21]

Within the latest surface-transportation-funding bill, SAFETEA-LU, there are over 200 requests for capital assistance, primarily for fixed-rail projects. The reality is that the federal transit assistance program cannot fund many of these requests and has to be selective about which projects to approve. With the encouragement of Congress and the White House, the Federal Transit Administration (FTA) has introduced a number of program initiatives to weed out ineffective projects. These initiatives include making cost-effectiveness a major criterion for rating these requests, and creating a Small Starts program to promote smaller, less costly projects to make scarce federal funds stretch further.

Capital Spending versus Customer Service

Until the flow of funding from the federal–aid program began to slow, most state transportation officials focused on only two objectives. One was committing all federal-aid funds obligated to the state. The second was meeting the schedule for awarding (letting) construction contracts. This reflected a focus on the highly leveraged nature of capital programs and on the local private contractors who were the major beneficiaries of these programs. Customer service, schedule or budget adherence, and cost-effectiveness were not considered critical since roadway users (and taxpayers) had no meaningful relationship with the agency.

Instead, these agencies remained protected behind a wall of federal regulations, design specifications, construction standards, and procurement and delivery processes. The upshot was a highly bureaucratic structure, without competition, innovation, customer focus, and public accountability. In many ways, this structure was like the Soviet command economy, characterized by lack of competition, low productivity, few service choices, rationing of what was produced and long waiting lines for service.

Demise of Fossil Fuel Taxes

It is scarcely news that fuel tax revenues are no longer expected to keep pace with the rising costs of preserving and expanding the nation's highway and public transit systems. This can be attributed to several factors:

- Increased fuel economy of vehicles, which reduces the gallons consumed per vehicle mile of travel.

- Higher fuel prices which tend to slow the growth rate of vehicle-miles-of-travel and sales of gas-guzzlers, like SUVs.

- Increased use of alternative power sources like ethanol, fuel cells, natural gas, hydrogen, and new-generation batteries.

- Increased availability of hybrid vehicles that further erode the consumption of fossil fuels.

- The reluctance of elected officials to increase motor fuel taxes for fear of being branded as "pro-tax" and incurring voter backlash.

Since fuel taxes are widely accepted and easily administered, it will be hard to replace them with other revenue sources, but it is unavoidable if the nation's transportation systems are to meet the demands of economic growth. Still, it's not going to happen any time soon, largely due to the large amounts of revenue fuel taxes continue to generate. According to a recent study, if tax revenues are limited to maintaining the surface transportation system at current service levels, we may yet be able to rely on motor vehicle fuel taxes for another 15 years. But that won't help us get highways restored more quickly, or reduce congestion.[22]

So the replacement process will gradually wean the public off of fuel taxes by introducing a number of alternative funding sources whose total revenues can more than offset lost fuel taxes. This could take a decade or more as existing vehicles are replaced and new technology is adopted to collect revenues through the direct pricing of roadway use, BTU consumption, or vehicle sticker prices.

Variable pricing addresses another issue fuel taxes leave unsolved: How to ration scarce lane space on roadway systems in densely developed metropolitan regions during periods of high demand. Right now, the system favors those who place a low value on their time, willing to wait in stop-and-go traffic for access to highway lanes.

The alternative is to charge for access to highway lanes, just as we charge for most other consumer services, with higher prices in force during periods of high demand. For instance, differential pricing rations the use of electric power, heating and cooking gas, drinking water and other essential goods whose production, like transportation, typically requires huge investments in capital plant and equipment.

The graphic below provides a typology of road-pricing approaches presently under consideration:

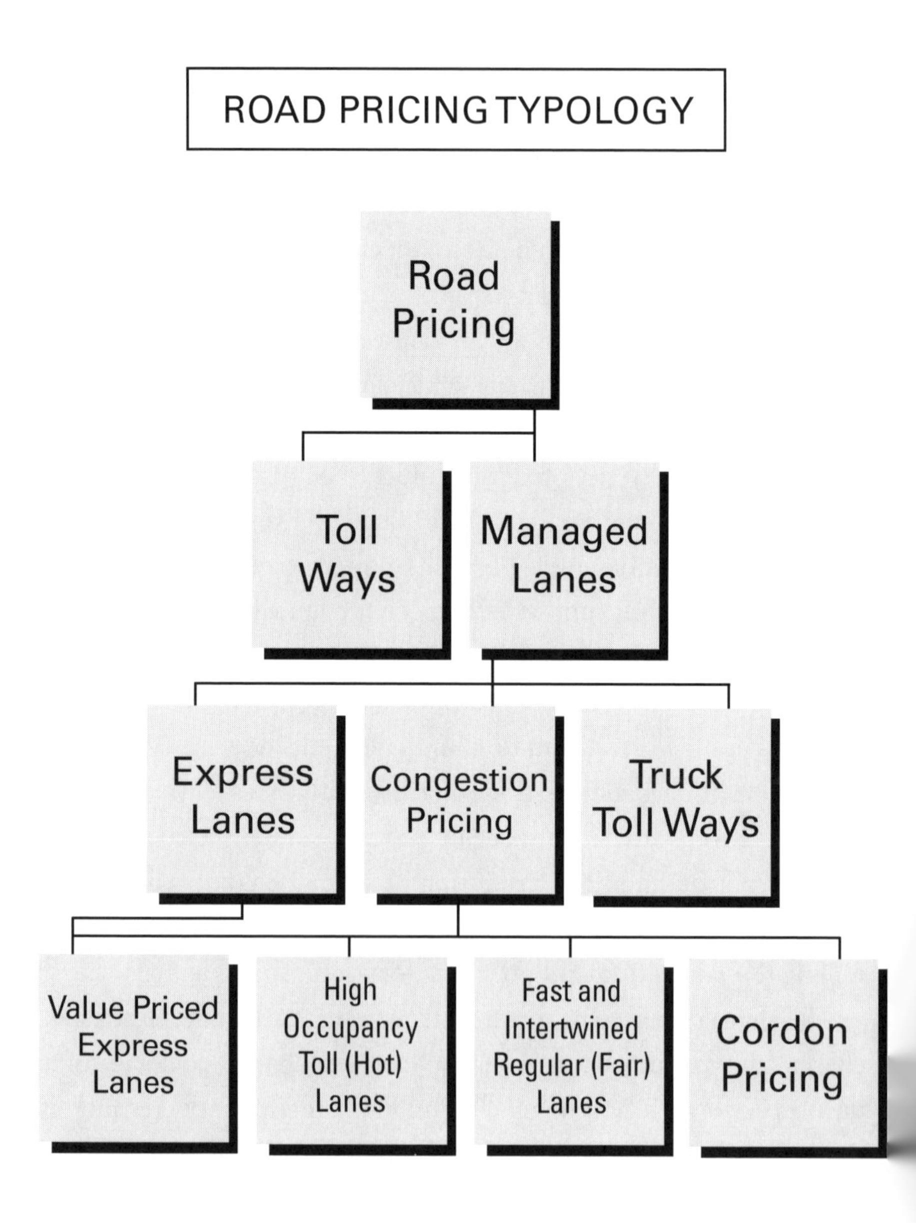

See Appendix A on page 231 for a definition of terms.

Since the cost and difficulty of adding lane capacity makes it impossible to provide universal price-free highway travel, it is inevitable that we will have to levy direct user charges in some form for some portions of the roadway system (particularly congested urban highways, parkways, and arterials where there is limited or no room to add capacity). Differential pricing can influence the driving habits of the public and freight haulers in ways that lead to more efficient use of the available capacity on existing transportation systems. Some motorists will choose to pay more for faster trips during times that make the most economic sense to them. Others will seek to save money by choosing to accept slower trip times on price-free roadways for their low-priority trips or shift their trips to periods of lower demand.

There is an interesting wrinkle to this that may bring a smile to many lips. As we saw earlier, electronic toll collection technology automatically charges motorists for highway use by debiting their prepaid account balances. In other words, the act of buying is divorced from the act of paying. And as savvy retailers know, this tends to mean that each customer buys more than if he or she had to worry about how much money they have in their pocket as they wander around the store – hence the widespread use of credit cards. Jargon-loving economists like to call this "lowering the price elasticity of demand."

The reluctance of elected officials to price highway use is in sharp contrast to how they treat public service utilities such as power (electricity, natural gas, or oil), water, and wastewater treatment. These utilities have raised revenues through direct user charges for years, often with variable pricing based on the level of demand at the time, day, or season of use. Highway use is treated differently because of the program's federal basis, as opposed to the state and local basis for the regulation of power, water, and wastewater treatment.

At the federal level, there is no public utilities commission established to set motor fuel tax rates for the federal highway program. The same applies to state and local fuel taxes, which are set by the state legislatures or local elected bodies. As a result, federal, state, and local elected officials are more visible and accountable for their actions regarding motor fuel taxes, which affect every constituent.

GASB 34 Requirements

One of the drivers of higher costs for surface transportation systems is the new accountability requirement to account for the current value and remaining service life of existing transportation facilities.

This resulted from issuance of Standard Number 34[23] by the Governmental Accountability Standards Board in 1999. It required for the first time that these two factors must be reflected in the annual financial statements of all state and local governments that own infrastructure by 2003 at the latest for new infrastructure and by 2006 at the latest for existing infrastructure built on or after 1980 for medium to large sized jurisdictions (but optional for smaller jurisdictions). Its intent was to recognize the future financial liability for renewing or replacing infrastructure assets.

As a result, the extent of the future financial liability for infrastructure asset renewal or replacement is publicly recognized through the annual financial reporting process to the public. This has made state and local jurisdictions that own transportation infrastructure more familiar with the future costs of preserving and replacing these assets. However, since most transportation agencies merely report the depreciation value of their infrastructure assets, there has been little advance in the application of life-cycle asset management principles by these agencies. The timeframe between application of these principles and the benefits they produce (such as lower lifecycle costs of the facility and less frequent replacement cycles) is simply too long relative to the standard election cycle for public officials.

And yet the positive benefit of financial visibility is the enhanced potential to securitize infrastructure assets. As noted earlier Chicago granted a 99-year lease on its Chicago Skyway toll road to a private consortium for an up-front payment of $1.83 billion. The condition and value of the asset was an important consideration, along with the cash flow from tolls over the term of the lease. As the Chicago Skyway deal shows, infrastructure securitization can convert a transportation facility from a sunk cost with future unfunded liabilities into an immediate cash bonanza for the facility's owner by enabling it to capitalize the facility's future earning potential through a long-term lease. This potential is maximized when the transportation facility has a direct revenue source like tolls or annual service payments from a public agency.

Institutional Inertia

Another challenge is stakeholders are resistant to change. These groups include those that have benefited from the traditional approaches used to plan, fund, and develop the nation's transportation system. Each has a vested interest in maintaining the status quo and tends to view any major change as threatening. For private sector transportation providers, the threat is to their financial welfare as well as their competitive position within their respective industries.

One-Size-Fits-All Approach to Project Development

To protect against corruption and abuse, federal and state governments instituted a variety of reforms in the early part of the 20th century that replaced the centuries-old way of doing things with uniform procedures for funding, financing, developing, and delivering highway infrastructure projects:

- The design and construction functions were separated by a Chinese wall. Design contracts were awarded on a negotiated "best-value" approach while construction contracts were awarded solely on the basis of the lowest responsible bid.

- Funding was focused on motor vehicle fuel taxes.

- Financing was limited to a "pay-as-you-build" approach that required all funding for a project to be in place before construction could begin.

Over time, additional requirements were added to accommodate an ever-increasing array of issues. These concerned environmental protection, social justice, labor protection, domestic industry protection, boycotting nations out of favor with U.S. policy, equal opportunity employment and contract incentives, public involvement, safety, security and most recently congestion relief. The entire highway program became layered with these agenda-based requirements that imposed specific processes for such functions as right-of-way acquisition, metropolitan and project planning, environmental clearance, and public involvement that were applied to all projects receiving any federal funds.

As a result, there was little flexibilty in how these requirements could be met, especially after the Interstate Highway Program began. With every new requirement came an additional layer of bureaucracy, consuming more of the available program funding while leaving less to develop and preserve infrastructure. While the national highway program became homogenized to ensure consistency of execution and administration, it lacked innovation, efficiency, and was unable to respond to consumer needs.

Bureaucratization of the Highway Program

The federal government's increasing involvement in funding and administering the nation's highway program resulted in what can best be described as a Soviet-style industry, as it took on many features characteristic of government-run monopolies that were neither efficient nor effective.

- **Government Monopoly:** Government control over the highway program through rules and regulations involving project funding, financing, procurement, and delivery that were administered by the state transportation agencies.

- **No Incentives for Innovation or Risk:** Bureaucratic focus on compliance with federal rules and regulations, with an emphasis on uniform product delivery to avoid the risk of losing funding eligibility by introducing more imaginative approaches.

- **Lack of User Pricing to Differentiate Service or Ration Available Highway Capacity:** The indirect nature of fund-raising through fuel taxes prevents market forces from capturing the economic value of accessibility provided by highway transportation facilities and leads to their overuse.

- **Uniformly Mediocre Products:** Little or no differentiation in service quality since all facilities are homogenous and all users are treated the same.

- **Perpetual Shortages:** Like the long bread lines that epitomized the ineffectiveness of the Soviet system, stop-and-go traffic congestion in and around the metropolitan areas epitomizes the ineffectiveness of the existing U.S. highway program.

- **User Satisfaction not a Consideration:** Oliver Twist had to content himself with the paltry amount of gruel he was served, and like him motorists have no alternative but to accept whatever level of service is provided by a highway program that is mainly preoccupied with bureaucratic rules and suffers from declining cost-effectiveness. They can never ask for "more."

- **The Construction Industry as the Primary Customer:** State transportation agencies are largely conduits of federal and state funds to local contractors. Since they receive most of the highway program's capital funds, local contractors continually pressure the agencies to spend all available federal funds, to keep the size of project contracts modest in order not to overburden their resource or bonding capacity and to meet the annual construction contract award schedule to maintain a stable flow of available capital funds.

- **Unachievable Long-Range Plans:** Highway capital plans routinely include more projects than can ever be funded to appease local elected officials. This is similar to the Soviet Union's five-year plans that could never be achieved due to a lack of realism about production and delivery but fed the pride of the relevant commissars.

- **Local Hoarding of Available Resources:** The deferred maintenance of major portions of the nation's highway system is due to state transportation agencies not using state-based resources to fund maintenance and preservation. They expected to receive future Federal Highway Trust Fund grants to rehabilitate, reconstruct, or replace facilities that wore out too quickly because of inadequate maintenance. Such hoarding of supplies at the source of production was one of the reasons for the failure of the Soviet Union's five-year plans.

In his farewell address before the U.S. Chamber of Commerce on July 6, 2006, Transportation Secretary Norman Y. Mineta said we need "a cultural change," to move from a government-monopoly command and control model toward greater involvement of the private sector and market forces.

In recent years the U.S. DOT and especially the FHWA leadership have spearheaded efforts to open up the federal-aid highway program to a much broader array of approaches in finance, contracting, right-of-way acquisition, safety, and most recently congestion relief using market-based pricing along special-purpose highway lanes.

Congestion relief is a major new focus of the U.S. DOT and FHWA. On May 16, 2006, Secretary Mineta launched a new *National Strategy to Reduce Congestion on America's Transportation Network*. This initiative includes demonstration projects for congestion pricing and variable tolling. Also, the FHWA's Value Pricing Pilot Program continues to provide grant funding for new approaches to congestion relief using variable pricing as well as such approaches as cordon-zone pricing, supported by new technology that eliminates much of the burden of paying direct user charges associated with most variable-pricing schemes.

More recently, the US DOT has established a new program to address the problems of rising congestion in the metropolitan regions of the nation with the Urban Partnership Agreements program. This program provides millions of dollars in seed money to encourage transportation planning and service agencies in metropolitan regions to work together to develop and implement plans to reduce congestion and improve the safety and mobility of transportation systems and services on a regional basis.

The challenge is to get state and local transportation authorities and federal division staffs to reinforce what the U.S. DOT officials in Washington are promoting to leverage scarce resources and increase competition between program and project service providers.

State Resistance to Applying GASB 34

Despite continuing efforts by FHWA to develop and promote a knowledge base for asset management, transportation agencies rarely choose to apply asset-management principles. For instance, a recent study found that only 21 out of 52 transportation agencies chose to respond to GASB 34 using the application of asset-management principles, practices, and systems.[24] Due to institutional inertia, the remaining 31 agencies instead chose the depreciation approach reporting the value of their infrastructure assets, which was easier for the accountants and financial analysts to understand and implement. Hence, most state DOTs avoided revealing the true nature of the condition and remaining service lives of their transportation facilities.

Highway Construction Industry Influence

The highway construction industry is one of the most powerful lobbying groups in the nation and is responsible for building the highway system we have today. It consists primarily of local construction companies who annually compete for projects funded by federal, state, and local, and occasionally developer funds. Most of these contractors are small companies that serve a particular region and rarely cross state borders. They are typically close to their state legislative representatives who approve transportation program budgets. They have invested in traditional equipment to construct roads and highways consistent with well-established construction specifications. This makes them wary of change, like new technical approaches and new alliances to pursue projects. All this has impeded efforts in many states to implement such alternative delivery approaches as design-build.

Similarly, where there are strong design or construction unions, there is often strong opposition to alternative project development approaches, such as public-private partnerships (PPP). The unfortunate fact is that the highway development industry is the source of a lot of institutional inertia.

Fixed Guide-way Industry Influence

Major transit fixed guide-way systems (heavy- and light-rail) are promoted by engineering, construction, and equipment manufacturers, or those who stand the most to gain from the funds spent up-front on these high-cost projects. They continue to be supported by urban transportation planners, environmental advocates, and urban politicians seeking the prominence afforded by these high cost, high capacity, and highly visible systems. With the potential for significant federal funding under the New Starts Program, the transit industry and their agency sponsors prefer the fragmented funding and delivery processes of the past and resist alternative concepts linked to the highway system.

This is why so little emphasis has been placed on HOT lanes or bus rapid transit (BRT), a form of commuter rail service without the rail that needs no separate fixed guide-way, power generation and distribution system, communications and signal systems, or sophisticated vehicles. But with the high cost of traditional fixed-rail projects and the tendency to overestimate patronage and underestimate costs, the fixed guide-way mentality impedes the transit industry's ability to adopt more cost-effective approaches.

Freight Carrier Productivity Concerns

Private-sector trucking, railroad, and air-cargo carriers (and the in-house goods movement operations run by some large manufacturing corporations) are usually driven by relatively narrow financial and customer-service concerns. They typically own their own trucks, railroad cars, or airplanes and some own infrastructure facilities like rail lines and truck terminals. Since deregulation, each of these industries has experienced significant change in their institutional environment and competitive positions.

Rapidly rising fuel prices also have seriously degraded their financial picture, forcing some firms into Chapter 11 bankruptcy or even liquidation. What these private-goods movement firms are most concerned about is reliability, travel time, facility condition, and operating costs. They are also very protective of their internal data on vehicle movements, volume of commodities moved, routing arrangements, and other data items that could be used to reveal their competitive position in the industry.

However, the financial pressures on private carriers is prompting greater interest in pooling resources to improve, expand, or develop inter-modal facilities or other infrastructure facilities that can yield public and private benefits. This is a departure from the past, especially for the private railroads, which typically avoided any involvement of public funding for fear of losing control of their facilities.

Fragmentation of Modes

When the typical engineer looks at surface transportation, he or she sees a collection of physically distinct modes. Since roadways, railroads, and waterways each have their own unique technologies and operating traditions, it is clear to the engineer that each mode exists in its own functional universe. Therefore, it is only logical that each mode should have its own unique institutional framework for their funding, planning, construction, and government support programs.

But when a marketing professional looks at surface transportation, he or she sees a very different picture. All modes have a common purpose, which is to serve the public by providing mobility for people and goods. The marketing professional believes that this common purpose far transcends any technical or operating differences between individual modes in the minds of transportation customers, who are only concerned with moving from here to there as quickly and as cheaply as possible. Therefore, all modes should operate as an integrated system to serve customers, and it logically follows that there should be a single institutional framework for funding, planning, construction, and government support programs.

It is scarcely a secret that the engineer's perception of things has traditionally carried the day, but it is becoming increasingly apparent that the marketing professional's perception is more realistic, and even necessary if transportation is to serve the American public in a sensible manner.

While there is some cross subsidy of public transportation from the Highway Trust Fund, the continued institutional fragmentation of surface transportation modes impedes efficient use of available surface transportation capacity. There are too many separate mode-oriented administrations, industries, funding sources and programs, a fact that ignores the common interests and needs that cut across the various modes, which in turn leads to poor use of infrastructure and resources. So the challenge is to weave together the various transportation modes in a manner that assures customers of reliable and timely service at a price that makes economic sense to both the customer and provider

Private freight carriers continue to operate as separate companies. Some of them, like CSX, Inc., have sought greater inter-modal integration by acquiring companies in these different modes. While private freight modes remain distinct, there is significant integration driven by innovations like containerization and shipper requirements for real-time tracking and dynamic routing to achieve just-in-time delivery of goods with minimal warehousing costs.

Diversity of Private Motor Carrier Industry

When highway transportation planners consider the changes in highway capacity and charging for it, they often fail to take into account the varied nature of the trucking industry, represented in the graphic below:

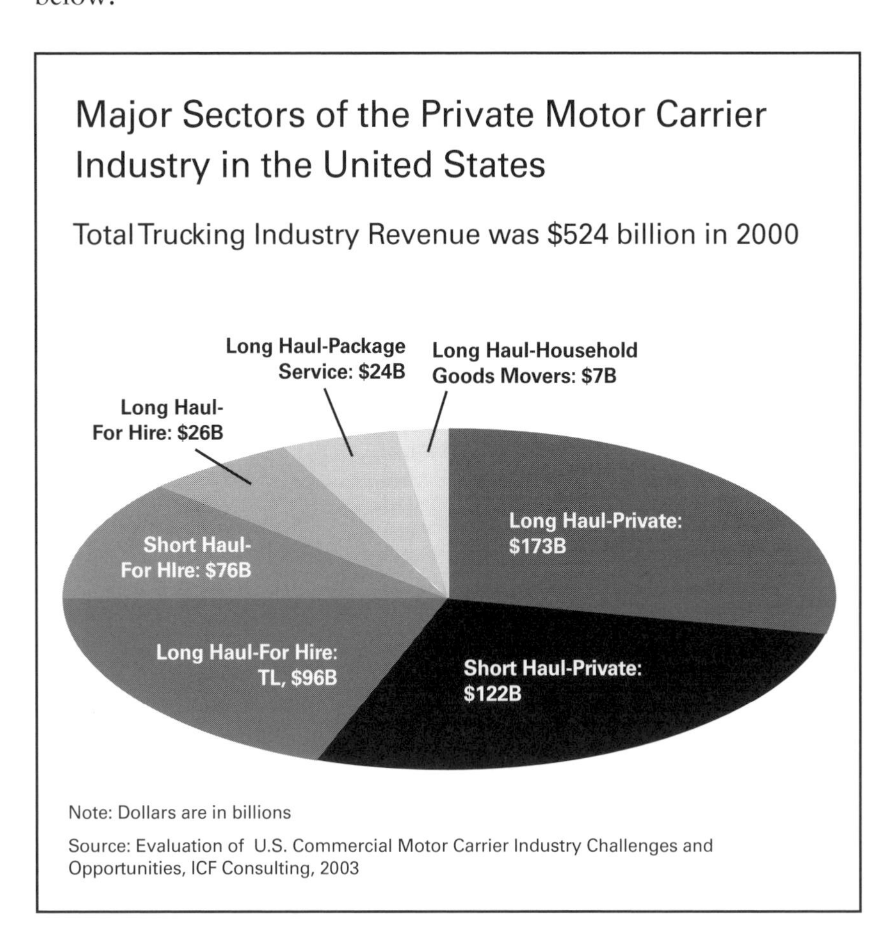

Note: Dollars are in billions

Source: Evaluation of U.S. Commercial Motor Carrier Industry Challenges and Opportunities, ICF Consulting, 2003

Some may view these individual sectors as examples of modal fragmentation. But they reflect prior economic regulations, service characteristics, ownership, and type of goods moved. In addition, cargo is often moved by companies representing several sectors, depending on the size of the shipment, length of haul, and the particular commodity. There are logistics firms that specialize in arranging for the intra-modal and inter-modal movement of shipments that are most cost-effective for the shipper.

The productivity, profitability, and competitive posture of each sector may be affected in different ways by congestion, HOV restrictions, changes in diesel fuel taxes, or imposition of direct user charges (especially on a segment-by-segment, time-of-day, or level-of-congestion basis). For example, while various sectors of the motor carrier industries have different ideas about the future of road pricing, common concerns include the following:

- **Adding tolls or road pricing to highway facilities without improving service.**

- **Placing tolls or congestion pricing on non-tolled lanes or local roads.**

- **Using toll revenues for non-facility specific or non-transportation purposes.**

- **Having to pay for both motor fuel taxes and tolls (the double taxation issue).**

- **Using variable toll rates for congestion management, thereby making toll costs unpredictable.**

- **Changing toll rates without advance notice**

- **Making tolls perpetual for the life of the facility.**[25]

The full spectrum of motor carrier industry sectors and how they are likely to interact with each other and other freight modes must be taken into account when considering changes to the transportation system, from an operations, capacity, and charging perspective.

Chapter 3:

Myths and Assumptions

Myths have an unfortunate tendency to cripple our imaginations. This can lead to the worst kind of unintended consequences, especially when such myths are based on assumptions about how the world *ought to be* rather than how it *actually is*.

Here's a real-world example of what this can mean:

Shortly after 7:30 on the morning on July 1, 1916, some 100,000 British soldiers climbed out of their trenches in France's Somme Valley, arrayed themselves in long lines against the morning sunlight, and began moving forward at a measured walking pace across No Man's Land towards the German trenches. They were fully confident they would achieve the long-sought breakthrough in the German lines that their officers assured them was bound to be a piece of cake.

The commanding general of the British Army in France was Sir Douglas Haig. He was a long-standing military professional, a member of the Scottish distilling family, and a Presbyterian fundamentalist who believed that he was in direct communication with God (an illusion that he shared with a surprising number of top military commanders throughout history).

The logic of his strategy for achieving victory on that brilliant July day seemed unassailable. It was based on the presumed effect of a week-long, round-the-clock, super-heavy British artillery barrage directed at the German trenches. The assumption was that this barrage would decimate the German soldiers occupying the trenches, destroy the barbed wire barriers in front of the trenches, and generally leave the German defenders helpless in the face of the overwhelming British attack.

In theory, Haig's strategy should have worked like a charm. But in practice, there were some problems.

- **Only 40 percent of the British artillery consisted of heavy guns. The rest were lightweight field pieces that could do little damage to trenches and barbed wire.**

- **Nearly one-third of the shells fired by British heavy guns failed to explode. This was because the British munitions industry had not yet come to terms with the need for quality control in shell production.**

- **The Germans housed most of their soldiers 30 feet below the trenches in elaborate dugouts that were impervious to even the heaviest artillery shells.**

So when the largely ineffective British artillery barrage finally ended at 7:20 that morning, the German defenders emerged from the dugouts with their ears ringing, but otherwise ready to withstand the British attack that the barrage had told them was coming. They quickly set up their Maxim machine guns, which could fire.30-caliber bullets at the rate of 600 per minute for hours on end. And as the British troops appeared in No Man's Land, began hosing the oncoming ranks with devastating fire that turned General Haig's strategy into a vain and costly myth.

By the end of that July day, the British Army had suffered the greatest single-day calamity in its history. More than 19,000 of its men lay dead in No Man's Land; over 38,000 had been wounded. This 57 percent casualty rate meant that nearly three out of every five of the 100,000 British soldiers who had gone over the top that morning had fallen victim to the myths on which General Haig had based his strategy (presumably after some long conversations with God), with little to show for it in the way of captured German territory.

As military historian John Keegan observed in his book *The First World War*:

> "There is nothing more poignant in British life than to visit the ribbon of cemeteries that marks the front line of 1 July 1916 and to find, on gravestone after gravestone, the fresh wreath, the face of a Pal or Chum above a khaki serge collar staring gravely back from a dim photograph, the pinned poppy and the inscription to 'a father, a grandfather and a great-grandfather.' The Somme marked the end of an age of vital optimism in British life that has never been recovered."[26]

The myths associated with American transportation may not cost as many lives as those from the Somme, but they cost a bundle in foregone economic activity due to transportation bottlenecks. Such costs can ripple across the nation to make us all less prosperous than we could be. And for too many Americans, "less prosperous" means a lot poorer, which is something we – and they – can ill afford.

We need to confront the myths associated with American transportation and understand how they can drain the life out of fresh ideas for improving mobility. Doing so can help to demystify them.

Ultimately, this promises a more productive discussion of better solutions to our transportation problems.

Surface Transportation Myths

Here are the key myths that influence decision makers and determine how the American public believes transportation should be provided, operated, paid for, and managed:

- Every American citizen has an inalienable right to unencumbered access to roadways without having to pay for them.

- Existing toll roads only need toll revenues to retire the debt originally issued to pay for their construction. Tolls should be removed once this debt has been paid off.

- Raising motor vehicle fuel taxes will cause a public outcry, lead to significant financial burdens for roadway users and cause drivers to seek other travel modes.

- More money is the only thing needed to solve our transportation problems.

- The process used to produce the Interstate Highway System over the past 50 years is fundamentally sound and should be continued.

- Public and private sector surface transportation stakeholders have distinct roles and responsibilities for providing and using transportation infrastructure. These should never be commingled.

- Private surface transportation modes like trucking and freight railroad companies are commercial enterprises that shouldn't receive public assistance.

- The public is preoccupied with traffic congestion.

- Private firms are only interested in quick profits when they participate in public-private partnerships for transportation. They can't be trusted to assume responsibilities for surface transportation traditionally provided by the public sector if these functions are to be performed in a manner consistent with established regulations, standards, specifications and concern for the public interest.

- The U.S. highway program is sufficiently competitive, market driven, and accountable to the public.

- Continued reauthorization of the existing surface transportation funding program is the most effective way to improve transportation.

The Problem With Assumptions

After 1918, Europeans, Americans, and their political leaders began to appreciate the full horror of World War I and the appalling magnitude of its casualties. So they turned their backs on the very concept of war, declaring that, "war is unthinkable."

But military professionals didn't have this luxury. After all, war was their business. And when they weren't actually engaged in it, they devoted considerable thought to what it could be like in the future.

Among these military professionals was a small group of visionaries who'd had experience with the primitive airplanes of World War I. Their experiences led them to think about the consequences of sending fleets of more modern airplanes to bomb the hell out of an enemy's factories, cities, and civilian populations in a future war.

These visionaries included General Hugh Trenchard of Great Britain, General Giulio Douet of Italy, and General Billy Mitchell of the United States. And during the 1920s, they gave birth to the concept of strategic bombing. They concluded that an enemy subjected to such treatment would have no choice but to surrender once its weapons-producing factories had been destroyed and civilian morale shattered by the effects of bombing. Such a war would therefore be short and avoid the years of stalemated trench warfare that had generated enormous casualties during World War I. These conclusions were generally accepted by Western political leaders and journalists; the sheer logic behind its assumptions was too compelling to ignore.

The most elegant version of the strategic bombing concept was developed by U.S. Army Air Corps theoreticians (the "Bomber Mafia") in the ivory tower academic atmosphere of the Air Corps Tactical School at Maxwell Field in Alabama, where the most promising young Air Corps officers received their graduate educations. It was called daylight precision bombing and was based on two critical assumptions:

- Fleets of modern heavy bombers (like the legendary B-17 Flying Fortress) could fight their way through to the enemy target and back home again without fighter escorts, experiencing only minimal losses in the process. Heavily armed with .50 caliber machine guns and flying in close formations to maximize their defensive firepower, the bombers would sweep aside all enemy fight opposition.

- The super-sophisticated bombsight developed by Swiss mechanical engineer Carl Norden would enable these bombers to hit individual factories and other military targets with pinpoint precision, sparing surrounding civilian areas form collateral damage.

But these assumptions were based on classroom logic and low-altitude bombing field experiments in the clear desert air of the American Southwest. When they had to face the reality of World War II over cloud-covered Germany, both assumptions collapsed.

During 1943, the U.S. Eighth Air Force based in the UK kept flying unescorted daylight bombing raids against targets in Germany. But determined opposition by the German Luftwaffe produced such staggering losses that only one 10-man bomber crew out of every five was likely to complete the mandatory tour of 25 missions.

Still they flew off each morning on missions to Germany laid on by their generals, who remained committed to the classroom myth of unescorted daylight precision bombing as a war-winning strategy.

By the end of 1943, U.S. Air Force generals reluctantly accepted the fact that unescorted daylight bombing was an empty myth, demolished by actual wartime experience. The sheer logic behind its assumptions was too compelling to ignore, but its basic assumptions could not survive the harsh glare of reality.

Surface Transportation Assumptions

As the story of U.S. daylight precision bombing strategy demonstrates, myths are too often based on sacred-cow assumptions that may be convenient, but have little basis in fact. Strategies based on such assumptions are always in danger of being blown out of the air when tactical managers actually try to execute them.

Efforts to improve American surface transportation have long been hamstrung by sacred cow assumptions that prevent the development of realistic solutions. They're too often used by tradition-bound stakeholders to perpetuate the institutional inertia that stifles the innovation needed to address national transportation needs.

Here are some of these sacred cows that should be relegated to the slaughterhouse:

- **Motor vehicle fuel taxes are the best funding source for surface transportation, and periodic tax increases can keep the Federal Surface Transportation Trust Fund solvent.**

- **Sharing funds across modes or between public and private transportation providers is impractical and counter-productive.**

- **It makes good sense to keep local land use and transportation decisions independent of higher levels of government.**

- **Direct user charges can't be placed on highways that were built with tax funds and that have not had tolls in the past.**

- The current proportion of federal funds for federal-aid capital projects (up to 80 percent) is the most sensible allocation of funding responsibility between the federal government and state or local governments.

- Federal funding can only be provided to individual transportation modes through explicit program formulas, Congressional earmarks, or special initiatives limited to pilot or demonstration programs.

- Use of federal funds for any portion of a transportation project should always require the application of all pertinent federal regulations to the entire project.

- Funds for capital construction, operations, and ongoing maintenance should be kept in separate, airtight categories. Block allocations of funding to individual transportation facilities are an impractical and counter-productive idea, as is allowing facility operators to determine how to use them.

- The most cost-effective way to deliver a transportation project is through the traditional design-bid-build approach.

- The activities of transportation agencies should continue to be limited to project planning, development, operations, and maintenance. Marketing and customer relations activities are best left to other stakeholders.

- **Public-private partnerships should never be used to displace public employees, especially those belonging to public employee unions and those filling political patronage jobs.**

A Final Note

Events like the first day on the Somme and our experience with daylight precision bombing may seem remote from today's transportation realities, but they overflow with lessons every strategic thinker should know by heart. Two that stand out are:

- **Myths should never be taken seriously, especially when they've become accepted as common sense. Like most fairytales, they contain much less than meets the eye. So much less, in fact, that it's usually a waste of time to do much more than dismiss them out of hand.**

- **Assumptions need to be based on more than logic if they're to be taken seriously. In fact, the more compelling an assumption's stand-alone logic, the more suspicious we should probably be of it. The acid test for any assumption is how well it stands up to the ice-water reality of hard facts.**

Chapter 4:

Questions, Questions, and More Questions

This chapter frames the issues facing surface transportation in America in terms of questions that can help us develop a new vision for what it should look like in the future.

These questions reflect current transportation problems, how they have been influenced by the Interstate Highway Program, the implications of the Federal Transportation Trust Fund, and commercial transportation deregulation during the past 50 years. They boil down information presented in previous chapters to address the challenges that an effective surface transportation vision must confront.

To keep us all on the same page, here is a brief summary of the challenges:

- Overcoming shortfalls in transportation capacity relative to travel demand. The resulting congestion on surface transportation facilities endangers the pace of national economic growth by diminishing mobility, accessibility, and productivity.

- Finding new and faster growing sources of transportation funding. Existing sources are no longer able to keep up with the mobility demands of an expanding domestic and global economy.

- Accommodating greater diversity among transportation customers and other stakeholders. Too many existing transportation programs seem to assume that we are still living in the Cold-War era.

- Determining which technological innovations transportation customers are willing to pay for and how they can be used to improve surface transportation.

- Identifying the management and institutional changes needed to reform the transportation status quo. This is an important step in placing improvement on a practical course to achieve the right kind of surface transportation vision.

Transportation Supports Economic Growth

Economic activity inevitably generates demand for transportation. The more economic activity there is, the greater is the demand to move people and goods.

In short, the nation's transportation systems provide essential support for the growth of its domestic economy and its competitive position in the global economy on which much internal consumption of goods is based. But this is likely to be complicated by the aging of the population. Older people are more dependent on services than goods.

The productivity gains in goods movement in the 1990s are largely attributable to commercial transportation deregulation, and private sector investment in better technology to expedite routing, tracking, and billing for individual shipments. Producer firms took advantage of this by replacing high-cost static warehousing of raw materials and finished goods with the kind of goods movement service that also provided short-term inventory functions. This is the whole basis of the just-in-time (JIT) delivery concept.

Internationally, the growth in containerization and the increase in container-ship sizes has increased efficiency and lowered the cost of global shipping. This supported the trend to relocate production facilities closer to sources of low-cost labor and materials in countries with lower taxes and less burdensome regulations on business firms. These trends are expected to accelerate. They will place increasing demands on American transportation, telecommunications, and other related services.

The question posed by these developments is:

- ***How will the capacity, condition, and operational efficiency of the nation's surface transportation system impact our economic vitality and competitive position in the global economy?***

Changes in the demographic composition of our population will have major effects on the choices we make about where to live and where to travel. The continued move from cities to the suburbs and the depopulation of rural America are increasing travel distances and times for commuters who continue to work in dense metropolitan regions, as they seek lower housing costs and better schools for their children.

Current trends indicate that as an increasing proportion of the GDP is generated by services instead of manufacturing, fewer people are commuting from the suburbs to central business districts and more are traveling cross-county or between counties. In addition, the growth of "edge cities" and the creation of "office campuses" in suburban areas is further changing the shape of traditional suburban life and commuting patterns that have been the main focus of public transportation systems, especially those based on heavy-rail technology.

The aging of the population along with the imminent retirement of the "baby-boomer" generation will see further depopulation in many areas of the Northeast, Midwest, and various rural communities. Retirees are more likely to seek housing in Florida, Arizona, North Carolina, Texas, and other Sunbelt states. This trend will continue despite the influx of younger immigrants with higher birth rates since their housing destinations tend to be in many of these same states, including Florida, Texas, and California.

The question posed by these demographic changes is:

- ***How will changes in population age, housing location choices, and travel patterns change the cost-effectiveness of traditional forms of surface transportation?***

It is important to understand the linkages between transportation availability and evolving economic patterns because it strikes at the heart of our future quality of life and prosperity that Americans will enjoy. So the various ways that commuters and businesses are adapting to worsening travel conditions and increasing congestion raises two critical questions:

- ***Are transportation customers sufficiently concerned by the current trends of mobility deterioration to insist that their elected officials develop something better?***

- ***Will these customers accept wholesale changes in transportation competition, pricing, accountability, and life-cycle asset management if such changes are the price of something better?***

The surface transportation establishment has generally ignored the traveling public, treating it more like an unavoidable nuisance rather than a prized collection of customers. The true customers of state and local transportation agencies have traditionally been the local construction companies that live off contracts from the surface transportation program. As a result, there has been little effort to help the general public understand how transportation is currently funded, how it is financed, and how it is operated and managed.

The "Golden Goose" that is the Transportation Trust Fund now appears unable to keep laying its golden eggs and supporting this cycle of construction contracts and political contributions. So the stewards of these programs – also its beneficiaries – have sought to convince the victims of this grossly inefficient system to trust them with more funding from higher motor vehicle fuel taxes.

However, the public no longer trusts them. They have suffered the mismanagement, the poor levels of service (traffic congestion), too many potholes, deteriorating bridges, and heard all of the "Chicken Little" claims that the whole transportation system is about to fall down unless more money is collected from the taxpayer, and they are loath to grant the keepers of the system more resources to waste.

And so, aside from the self-serving companies that develop and deliver transportation infrastructure and systems, few are willing to expand the status quo when it comes to funding, management, and the application of technology. They are looking for credible program sponsors to demonstrate they can be trusted to deliver greater value for any increases in surface transportation funds.

It is not clear that a credible case has yet been made to convince a skeptical public that more money alone will solve the nation's surface transportation problems. What is needed is bolder thinking that completely overhauls or even replaces current programs. But the many corporate and political stakeholders who benefit from the status quo are a major impediment to any substantive actions in this direction. They constitute the institutional inertia that prevents necessary changes from taking place.

Diverse Transportation Stakeholders

There is a common misconception among planners and politicians that the U.S. surface transportation system serves a homogeneous group of users. For example, most transportation planners focus on peak-period commuters while treating goods movement as a secondary consideration.

In reality, transportation users are a highly diverse group of commercial organizations and individuals who use the system in different ways. These users therefore are sensitive to different aspects of transportation costs, convenience, reliability, safety, emissions and operations.

These stakeholders include:

- Private automobile drivers making trips for commuting, shopping, recreation, and children's taxi purposes.

- Trucking firms, including in-house service fleets, commercial for-hire trucking companies providing truckload or less-than-truckload services, independent owner-operators, pick-up-and-delivery services, express package services, household goods movers, and specialized goods movers.

- Commercial freight carriers that compete with the highway-based trucking industry. These include freight railroads, air cargo firms, barge and towing operators using inland waterways, and ocean-going ships.

- Public transportation service providers that use buses, heavy-rail, light-rail, commuter rail, bus rapid transit, and social service vans to move people.

- Special interest groups concerned with issues affecting the natural environment, community and historic preservation, and other social agenda.

- Private land owners and developers whose property values and development potential are affected by the increased accessibility provided by nearby surface transportation facilities.

- Elected officials and public policy-makers whose popularity and political future depends on how the public perceives the success or failure of transportation programs and projects.

By limiting the discussion and consideration only to the needs of a few obvious stakeholders, the process of developing the necessary consensus for surface transportation visions, policies and strategic plans is badly skewed and ends up going nowhere.

This leads to the question:

- ***How effective are stakeholder outreach and coordination efforts in developing a consensus on the nation's future surface transportation needs and what kind of strategies can meet these needs in a cost-effective manner?***

Competition Within the Industry

There is intense competition among those companies that develop transportation infrastructure as well as among those carriers that provide freight services on these facilities. There is also modal competition between transit providers and the individual automobile like taxis for moving people in metropolitan areas.

Such competition encourages providers to offer better services by focusing on customer needs and performance by adopting more efficient production methods to keep their prices within sensible economic bounds, by introducing new technologies that promote better operating efficiency, and by keeping their equipment and facilities in a state of good repair to maximize reliability. (At least in theory. It may be difficult to find many Boston transit riders and taxi customers who agree.)

This is in stark contrast to the lack of competition among most highway agencies that have been protected from competition by dedicated funding sources, monopoly authority over highway development and operations, and federal and state statutes defining their roles and responsibilities, for project financing, procurement, and delivery.

Exceptions to this can be found among those operators of toll roadway facilities who must compete daily for customers with toll-free roadways. To justify the added costs to motorists of their tolls, these operators must offer increased customer value in terms of faster travel times, greater reliability and safety, smoother ride quality, and other service amenities. During the past 15 years, competitive strength has been enhanced by the introduction of electronic toll collection technologies that have enabled toll facility operators to move in the direction of eliminating the need for motorists to slow down and often wait in line to pay tolls.

Greater competition offers the potential for enhancing service quality, customer responsiveness, and cost-effective technological innovations. But turning potential into reality can be a major management challenge.

The following questions are directed to members of Congressional study commissions, Congress, state governors and legislators, and managers of state and local transportation agencies:

- ***How can greater competition be incorporated in highway programs to encourage more cost-effectiveness, more technological innovation, better service quality, greater performance accountability, and better facility stewardship?***

- ***How can traditional surface transportation programs be changed to reduce bureaucratic inertia and to promote greater competition, value-based pricing, innovation, and life-cycle stewardship to achieve the benefits of cost-effectiveness, responsiveness, and accountability that are the hallmarks of successful firms and industries in a capitalist society?***

Deregulating the Highway Program

As noted above, the nation's highway program is hamstrung by regulations involving funding and financing, procurement, and project delivery. And then there are a host of special provisions, like Davis-Bacon wage rules, "Buy America" requirements and protracted environmental clearance processes.

All this inhibits competition and increases program and project costs, which exacerbate the challenge of meeting surface transportation needs. As one of the few remaining publicly sanctioned monopolies (Major League Baseball being another), the nation's highway program lacks incentives to change, improvise, improve, and thus free itself from a status quo that is no longer economically viable.

These issues raise the following questions:

- ***What statutory and regulatory changes are needed to unleash the competitive spirit in the highway development program in the U.S. and make the program more cost effective, customer responsive, and technologically enabled?***

- ***How can the U.S. move from a "Soviet-Style" to a "Capitalist-Style" highway program that reflects the free-market principles of competition, value-based pricing, accountability, and long-term asset stewardship?***

Integration Among Transportation Modes

We have already discussed this, but it's worth pounding the table about it again.

Each transportation mode seems to exist within its own functional universe regarding institutional, financial, operational, and technical factors. This results from inherent differences in how and when each mode evolved, from the relative roles and responsibilities of the public versus the private sectors, from the extent to which funding is provided by taxes versus private investment, and from the needs of customers.

The private sector carriers that own their own infrastructure (railroads) and equipment (railroads and trucking firms) have long resisted public involvement, even public funding since certain strings are attached to its use.

Public-sector transportation agencies reinforce modal fragmentation by having separate administrations within the U.S. DOT with responsibility for highway, transit, railroad, aviation, maritime, motor carrier safety, pipeline safety, and rail/truck/pipeline rate issues. Most state departments of transportation mirror the same modally fragmented organization structure.

But transportation consumers do not see the world the way transportation authorities do. Rather, they integrate these different modes as a matter of fact during the course of the daily lives. For instance, there is the commuter who drives to a commuter-rail station's parking facility to take a train into the office. Or there is the logistics company that arranges for a container to be off-loaded intact at a port terminal at an ocean shipping port like Los Angeles, loaded on a premium-service double stack train for the long-haul portion of its overland trip to the American heartland, and then reloaded onto a truck for its final delivery to its destination.

That is to say, the organizational, institutional, financial, operational, and technical fragmentation of the American transportation system is not in line with the reality of how these modes are actually used by customers. This creates artificial and inefficient barriers to move people and goods.

Although several past Secretaries of Transportation have elaborated on the virtues of a fully integrated set of modal administrations within DOT to enhance its efficiency and effectiveness, the rhetoric never matched reality inside DOT's headquarters or the division and field offices. The most obvious fragmentation within the U.S. DOT occurs in surface transportation, where the roadway and public transportation programs and funding are overseen by separate and often competing administrations (FHWA and FTA).

Given the scarcity of resources to support the federal government's various mode-specific programs, plus the customer's insistence on regularly crossing borders between the modes, and the growing need for more logistical integration in the future, the question for current policy-makers is:

- ***How can greater cost-effective integration of various transportation modes be achieved across the board while recognizing their obvious differences in ownership (public versus private), operating characteristics, jurisdictional responsibility, and funding sources?***

Public and Private Sector Roles in Multi-Modal Systems

For many decades, the federal, state, and local administrators and private sector commercial carriers have maintained well-defined distinctions in their respective roles and responsibilities.

Public-sector transportation agencies allocate and spend public funds, oversee program administration, project procedures, regulatory oversight for safety, and approve certain rates and mergers involving private railroad and trucking companies.

Privately owned trucking companies and intercity and regional bus companies use roadways provided by the public sector. They own or lease the vehicles they use to move goods and people. Freight railroads own or lease their rail lines, locomotives, and freight cars (though several companies may share the use of these assets through formal agreements).

From the late 1880s until 1980, government sought to control the rates, routes, and services of private carriers through economic regulation. The laws and administrative bureaucracies this spawned included:

- Regulation of the railroad industry in 1887 to prevent monopolistic abuses in service pricing and competition.

- Passage of national anti-trust laws in 1890 to prevent market abuses caused by monopoly power within large private industries like oil.

- Regulation of the emerging for-hire trucking industry in 1935 to provide an economic framework for service pricing and competition to avoid rate-setting abuses by larger carriers, and to protect existing carriers by restricting the issuance of certificates for operating authority to new firms.

- Regulation of the fledgling airline industry by the Civil Aeronautics Board in 1938 to control rates, routes, and passenger schedules.

Economic regulation of privately owned common carriers was government's way to address abuses resulting from the monopolistic tendencies inherent in highly capital-intensive industries. But by the 1970s, economic regulation had itself become the primary inhibitor of competition, innovation, and efficiency. The established members of regulated transportation industries were freed of true competition and prohibited from exercising marketing, pricing, and technology innovations to lower the cost of transportation services to customers. In effect, economic regulation served to protect the established carriers who were neither efficient nor innovative.

Such economic regulation was largely eliminated in the 1970s and 80s. For the most part, this resulted in significant price reductions to customers while enhancing productivity through operating improvements and technological innovation.

Since the end of regulation, government transportation agencies have focused on allocating public funds, program administration, project procedures, oversight of safety regulations and certain rate and merger issues involving freight railroads and truck companies. Private trucking companies and intercity and regional bus companies continue to use the transportation infrastructure provided by the public sector. Major railroads continue to own their infrastructure. And most commercial carriers own their equipment.

Inter-modal and multi-modal operations were spurred on by freight containerization and by the escalating growth of imported goods that needed to be moved from ports-of-entry to internal distribution centers, or directly to customers operating on just-in-time delivery schedules. As a result, the nation entered a period of unparalleled growth in the volume of domestic freight movements. Logistics managers and companies are facilitating the integration of private sector carrier operations to expedite goods movements in ways to better meet customer needs.

But public sector transportation agencies have been less successful in developing multi-modal strategies through cooperative planning and financial partnership arrangements with private firms. This can be attributed to two major factors:

- The institutional fragmentation of public sector transportation programs and funding along strictly modal lines.

- Continuing distrust between the public sector transportation agencies and private sector carriers due to the legacy of government regulation.

These two factors explain why so few efforts have been made to develop cross-modal project planning and fundsharing as a means of addressing capacity bottlenecks and other operating inefficiencies that continue to hamper all modes of transportation.

So, we're left with another fundamental question:

- ***What kind of policies and institutional relationships are needed for public transportation agencies and private sector carriers to find common ground so they can*** *cooperatively address inter-modal and multi-modal bottlenecks that result in operating inefficiencies and declining customer service?*

Public and Private Sector Roles in Highways and Transit

Early in the 20th century, an effort to end a pattern of abuses involving public transportation agencies and the private companies they hired became so outrageous that it resulted in wholesale reforms and regulations. One consequence of this was the pervasive balkanization and bureaucratization of the project development process. Today, public agencies are responsible for project sponsorship, concept development, preliminary planning, funding and financing administration, preliminary design and environmental administration, acquisition of needed parcels and permits, contract procurement, and administration of a project's final design, construction, construction inspection and materials testing.

Private firms, on the other hand, are responsible in most states for providing design services through a separate qualifications-based negotiated contract, and a separate contract is awarded for the construction phase to a contractor on a lowest bid basis. This multi-step project delivery method is called "design-bid-build" or DBB. Other private firms are also retained for quality control services, construction inspection, and sometimes materials testing.

This fragmented process for delivering highway projects was used during most of the 20th century and continues pretty much intact today. It is inflexible, inefficient, and slow to adopt technological innovations that could improve productivity and performance. This is perpetuated by keeping most project construction contracts modest enough not to overburden smaller, local contractors that lack the resources or the incentive to innovate. This whole process stands in sharp contrast to the collaborative efforts of the public and private sectors before 1900 to develop infrastructure projects.

Reversing this approach and encouraging greater involvement by the private sector in public project delivery began during the Vietnam War. The rapid expansion of the war effort demanded more base housing be quickly designed and built for soldiers and their families as quickly as possible. To expedite this process and reduce the cost of the delivered product, the Department of Defense turned to the design-build (DB) process, which combined the design and construction functions under a single contract.

This enabled the DB team to integrate their respective functions better, thereby reducing design errors and enabling more concurrent processing of the project development process, which allowed for faster delivery. Subsequent budget challenges encouraged the Defense Department to adopt asset management practices to achieve lower life-cycle infrastructure costs.

In the 1990s, the Federal Transit Administration (FTA) became an early proponent of public-private partnerships (PPP) within the U.S. DOT. It approved several public transit fixed guide-way projects that used the PPP approach to expedite project delivery while transferring certain cost and schedule risks to the private sector partner. The PPP processes included design-build and design-build-operate-maintain (DBOM).

Transit systems deliberately under-price their fares to provide such social benefits as serving the mobility needs of people who can't afford automobiles or who live in densely-populated areas like the New

York metropolitan region where high-capacity fixed rail systems are the only way to accommodate travel demands during commuting periods. Primarily, PPPs have been used to manage the costs and risks of large-scale projects rather than to attract outside financing that could be repaid from project proceeds. Currently, out of 39 New Starts transit capital projects approved by FTA since 2000, only 7 are considered PPP projects and most of these are for design-build project delivery approaches.

More recently, the FHWA has promoted the concept of public-private partnerships to leverage scarce public resources for essential highway projects that could not otherwise be developed using traditional approaches. FHWA has also instituted Special Experimental Project programs (SEP-14 and SEP-15) that enable project sponsors to experiment with alternative ways to plan, finance, contract, acquire right-of-way, and streamline the environmental clearance process consistent with NEPA.

Both FHWA and FTA are helping state and local sponsors and their private sector partners to innovate and optimize their programs. Currently, 20 states and Puerto Rico have passed legislation authorizing the use of PPPs for transportation projects. Another 5 have pending legislative action on PPPs, as shown in the graphic on the page 138.

A surrogate measure of state willingness to pursue alternative project delivery approaches to leverage scarce public resources for surface transportation projects is the number of states with the authority to use design-build contracts. The graphic on page 139 shows that 33 states currently have full authority to use DB, while an additional five states have authority to use DB under certain circumstances.

Most of the state transportation agencies continue to follow traditional approaches to project development, funding, and delivery. Only a few states are implementing major changes to their programs,

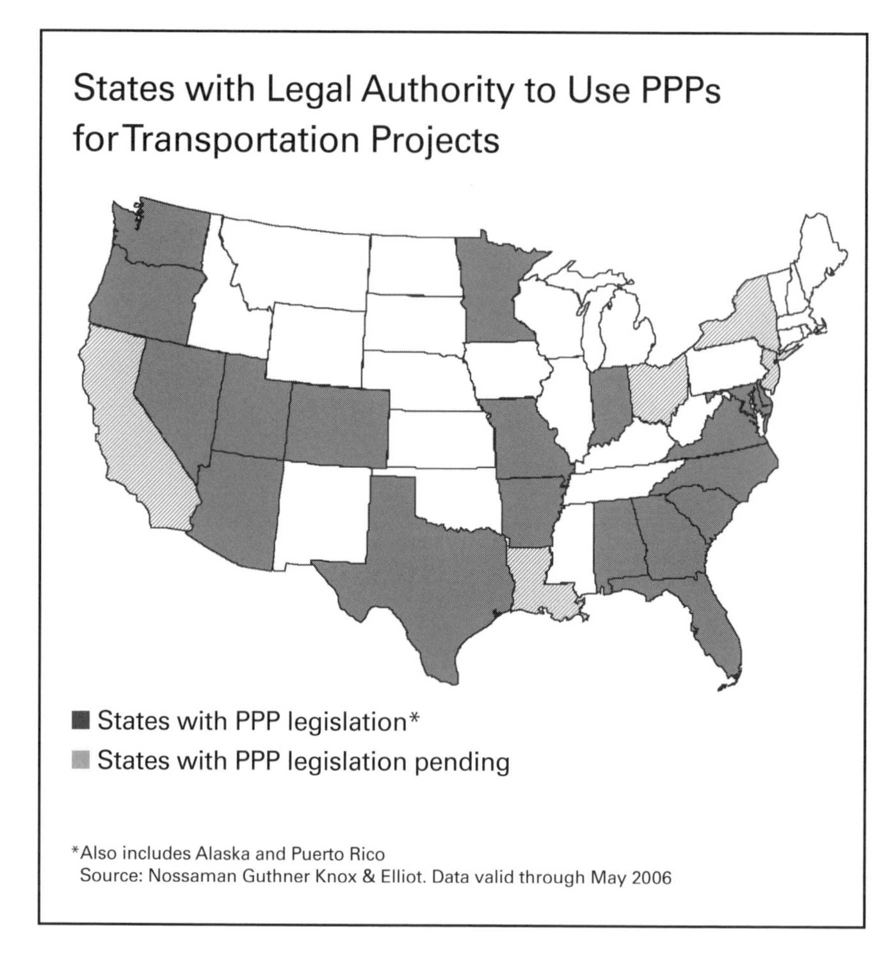

despite 20 state legislatures passing bills permitting the use of PPPs.

This raises two questions:

- *As more funding and program administration responsibility is shifted from the federal government to state and local governments, how much freedom should state and local transportation agencies have to assign more responsibilities, risks, and rewards for individual projects to private-sector partners?*

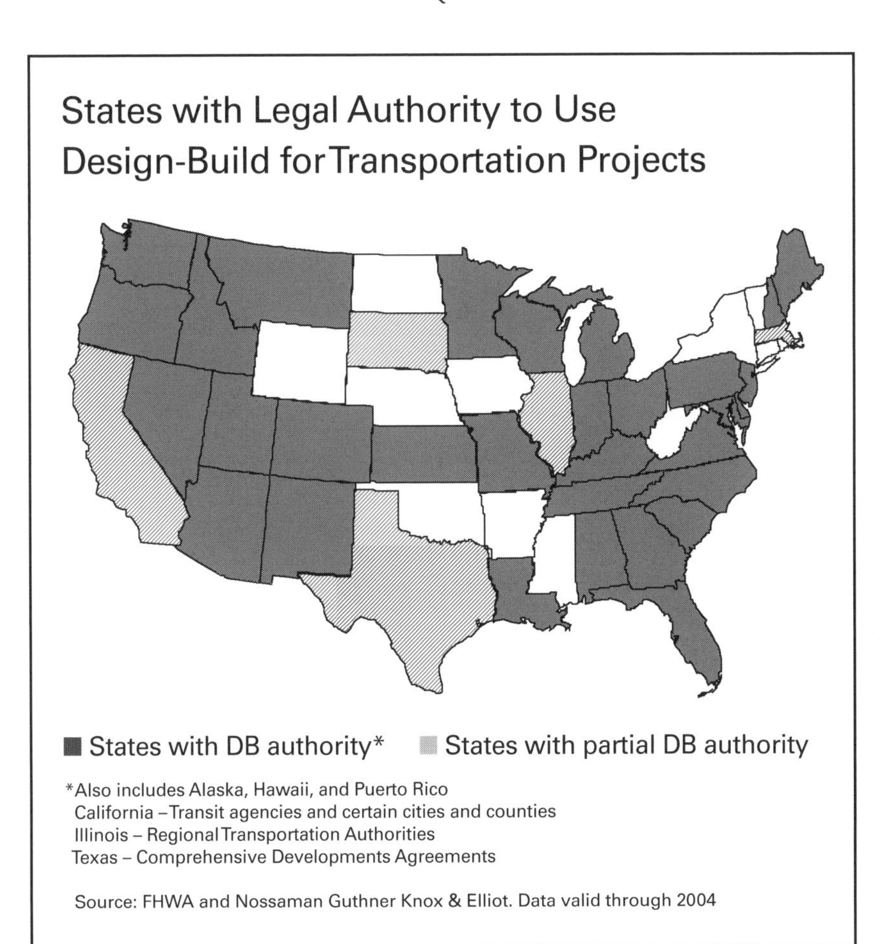

- ***In a PPP, which parties should be responsible for ensuring that the broader public interests are protected?***

Another index of private sector involvement in surface transportation projects is the number of states that use or are considering using the concession form of PPP, where most of the roles, responsibilities, risks, and rewards are assumed by the private sector concession team. Such arrangements can be either long-term leases of existing facilities, or the development, financing, and preservation of new facilities.

In most cases, concession projects involve tolled facilities.

The following exhibit shows the states where concessions currently exist or are being considered. As indicated below, 7 states currently have concession-led projects while another 19 are considering them. There are currently 74 concession projects in the project consideration or proposal pipeline within the U.S.

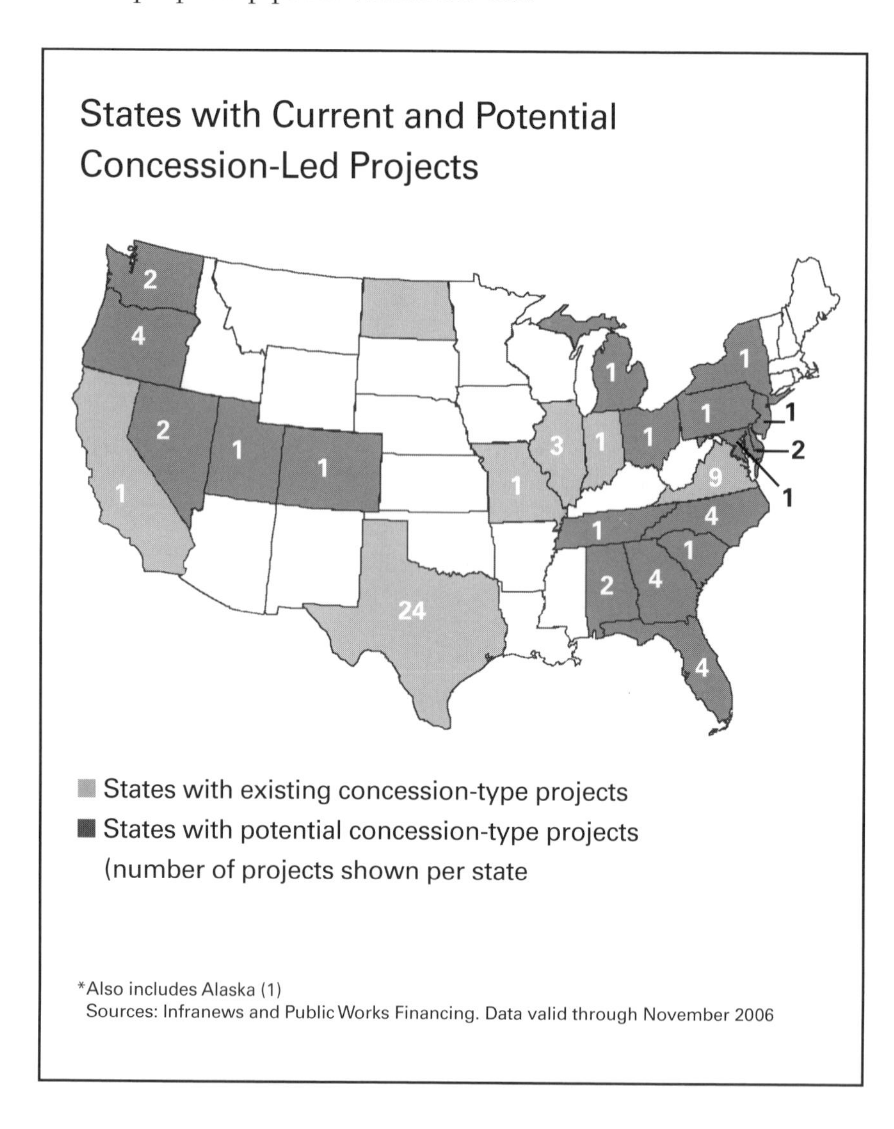

Allocating Authority and Responsibility

Federal funding of roads began with the Federal-Aid Road Act of 1916, after decades of debate over what role the federal government should have in funding and regulating the nation's roadways. The Federal-Aid Highway Act of 1956 produced the Interstate Highway Program. The ensuing funding formulas, program rules and regulations, and policies and procedures became almost standardized throughout the highway development program as states receiving federal funds tended to emulate the federal program, particularly for Interstate projects.

But now, the continuing shift of responsibility for funding, program development and administration from the federal government to state and local governments poses the following questions:

- *With less funding for the nation's surface transportation program coming from the federal government, to what extent should Congress and the U.S. Department of Transportation shift more funding and program administration authority to state and local governments?*

- *What is the federal interest in the nation's surface transportation system?*

- *Should the federal government limit its responsibilities only to those elements of the national surface transportation program where there is a clear national interest?*

- ***What should the roles of Congress and the U.S. DOT become if the federal government limits its focus on those aspects of the surface transportation program and system where there is a clear national interest?***

These questions need to be addressed by all stakeholders, customers as well as providers, in the nation's various transportation systems and modes. But to answer these questions in a sensible manner will require stakeholders to focus on a common vision for how transportation systems should be structured, funded, financed, administered, operated, integrated, and maintained.

These driving questions are the focus of the next chapter, along with a discussion of possible strategies for moving towards a suitable surface transportation vision.

Chapter 5:
Surfing for Strategy

It's often said that, "management is about getting things done right. Leadership is about choosing the right things to do."[27]

An example of how poor leadership choices can wreck the impact of brilliant management is the spectacular bombing raid on Pearl Harbor by Japan's Imperial Navy on the morning of December 7, 1941. It destroyed the U.S. battleships *Arizona* and *Oklahoma*, disabled the battleships *California, Nevada,* and *West Virginia*, and inflicted severe damage on the battleships *Maryland, Pennsylvania,* and *Tennessee.*

But it left untouched Pearl Harbor's fuel storage and ship repair facilities. This enabled Pearl Harbor to continue operating as a full-service forward naval base aimed like a dagger at the heart of Japan's military ambitions in the Central and Southwestern Pacific.

Had Pearl Harbor been crippled as a naval base, the U.S. Pacific Fleet would have been forced to retreat 2,000 miles to the West Coast of the United States where it could no longer threaten Japan's ambitions. And during the year or more it would take to rebuild Pearl Harbor, Japan had at least an outside chance of negotiating a settlement with a dispirited United States that gave it free reign throughout the western Pacific. Achieving such a settlement was Japan's only possibility for meaningful victory in the Pacific War.

So, despite the managerial brilliance of the Imperial Navy's sea commanders in doing things right, its leaders failed to choose the right things to do in planning the Pearl Harbor raid. And this made Japan's defeat inevitable.

Are we going to make the same kind of wrong-target mistakes when it comes to choosing the right things to do in developing a vision for American transportation in the future?

To avoid such mistakes, we need to focus on 10 driving questions for defining a sensible strategy. They concern both short-term and long-term strategies for moving forward, to achieve the right kind of surface transportation vision and to meet the key challenges of changing current well-established surface transportation programs.

These 10 driving questions need to be addressed before we try to strategize about the future of surface transportation in America. They're intended to motivate some critical soul-searching among public and private sector leaders to produce intelligent choices about the right things to do to fix the transportation mess we're in.[28]

1. *Where are we today in terms of adequate surface transportation and how did we get to this point?*
2. *What needs fixing and what priority order should we assign to these fixes?*
3. *What should the nation's surface transportation systems look like in 20 to 30 years?*
4. *What kind of policies and strategies can help achieve this vision?*
5. *How do we measure whether the vision is being achieved?*
6. *What short-term and long-term actions should we take to move from our current situation to a shared vision of transportation stakeholders?*
7. *What are the fundamental principles that should be*

followed in developing and executing a new vision for surface transportation?

8. *What policy, program, or process changes already underway would support the concepts of the new vision for surface transportation?*
9. *What is likely to hold the nation back in achieving the vision for transportation and what can stakeholders and sponsors do to overcome these barriers?*
10. *How can new and emerging technologies help address the fiscal, congestion, and safety challenges of achieving the new vision for surface transportation in America?*

These questions transform the process from one of incremental, glacial change as embodied in SAFETEA-LU to a more radical reinvention of the entire surface transportation program. They recognize the urgency of the challenges facing our nation as an ever increasing diversity of transportation stakeholders move into an era of rapid shifts in global trade, political alliances, security threats and technological innovation.

Defining a Vision

Early in 1941, the government of resource-poor Japan realized that it needed to seize control of the petroleum and other raw material sources in the Dutch East Indies (now Indonesia), French Indochina (now Vietnam and Cambodia), and the Malay Peninsula (now Malaysia). But this would require neutralizing the offensive threat posed by the U.S. Navy's Pacific Fleet based at Pearl Harbor. The government assigned this task to the Imperial Navy, whose Combined Fleet was headed by Admiral Isoroku Yamamoto.

It's now clear that the Imperial Navy had two strategic alternatives for neutralizing the U.S. Pacific Fleet. One was to cripple the fleet itself through a direct attack on its warships, or cripple Pearl Harbor's ability to function as the fleet's forward base in the Pacific.

Crippling the U.S. Fleet would require disabling the eight battleships that made up the fleet's traditional battle line. But to be really successful, this alternative would also require disabling the two brand-new U.S. battleships then assigned to its Atlantic Fleet (which could be quickly reassigned to the Pacific), along with the three aircraft carriers assigned to the Pacific Fleet and the three carriers in the Atlantic. It would also have to find some way to slow down the U.S. Navy's massive warship construction program that was already building eight more battleships and 10 more aircraft carriers, expected to enter service beginning in late 1942. Quite a tall order.

The most effective way to cripple Pearl Harbor's ability to function as a naval base would be to destroy its fuel storage and ship repair facilities. Without them, the U.S. Pacific Fleet would have to return to the U.S. West Coast, where it could no longer deter Japanese military expansion in the Western and Southwestern Pacific during the year or so it would take to rebuild Pearl Harbor.

> It soon became apparent that the basics of either strategy could be carried out through a surprise air raid launched by a task force built around the Imperial Navy's six first-line aircraft carriers. Details of such a daring raid were already being developed by Commander Minouru Genda, one of the world's most gifted naval tactical planners, who was convinced that it could be made to work. This left Admiral Yamamoto with the choice of which strategic target to focus on.
>
> Yamamoto had a reputation as an expert poker player, gained during his years of study at Harvard and as an Imperial Navy naval attaché in Washington. So he looked at the four aces in his hand and placed his bet: Attack the warships of the U.S. Pacific Fleet that were moored each weekend in Pearl Harbor. But the U.S. Navy had the equivalent of a royal flush. This meant that Yamamoto had chosen the wrong target and lost the poker game.

It's vital that we avoid making the same kind of mistakes in developing an effective vision and strategy for the future shape of surface transportation in America. So we have to make sure that we choose the right targets. This means that we must begin by addressing three core questions.

1. ***Where are we today in terms of the adequacy of transportation infrastructure and services, and how did we get to this point?***
2. ***Given the current transportation situation, what needs fixing and what priority order should we assign to these fixes?***

3. Looking 20 to 30 years ahead, what should the nation's transportation systems look like in terms of:

- The purposes served by surface transportation.
- Transportation choices and competition.
- Transportation capacity and use.
- Transportation service quality and accountability.
- Effective integration through multi-modal and intermodal coordination.
- Resources available to improve transportation and our ability to use them in the most cost-effective manner.
- The self-sufficiency of transportation funding sources and the efficiency of available financing mechanisms.
- The authority and responsibilities of federal, state, and local governments over publicly owned and operated transportation facilities.
- The involvement and stewardship of the private sector in transportation.
- Protecting and enhancing the nation's major metropolitan regions, which generate most of its Gross Domestic Product.
- The strength of our competitive position within the global economy through interstate and international transportation and trade.

Once we define the features of this vision, bringing them to life will require that we address two other questions.

4. What policies and strategies can enable us to achieve this vision during the next 20 to 30 years?

5. *How can we measure the extent to which the vision is being achieved?*

Moving Towards a Vision

Defining this vision demands that we understand the current problems facing the nation's surface transportation systems, how these issues are likely to evolve, and the consequences if left unchecked.

It also requires that we extrapolate recent trends and project future developments that will affect the provision and use of transportation modes. The key drivers of change in the provision and use of transportation include transformations in the size and composition of the nation's population, domestic and global economic activity and their inter-dependencies, modal features and service choices based on new technologies and investment, and user demands for improved mobility based on changing individual lifestyles, work habits, and business practices. These include:

- Increased demands for personal mobility and better transportation service.

- Number of senior citizens who remain active, retire later, and have needs that are different from those of younger citizens.

- Increasing environmental awareness and the need to conserve natural resources.

- An increase in the diversity of workforce and market, including niche markets served by mass customization of manufacturing processes and delivery services.
- Faster pace of life via cell phones with global reach, telecommuting and virtual offices, wireless computing, and internet services for marketing, shopping, banking, and bill-paying.

- Smaller households composed of single people and married couples with no children, which make urban living more attractive and provide a resurgence of mixed-use residential/retail/commercial communities in metropolitan regions.

- Vehicle specialization serving multi-purposes, leading to an increase in auto ownership per registered driver.

To maintain our competitive position in the world's economy and provide enhanced mobility to serve the demands of our diverse population and industry means replacing today's outdated approach to transportation funding, financing, delivery, and bureaucratic administration.

A new strategy would include an integrated set of self-sustaining and resource-conserving funding and financing mechanisms, more cost-effective ways to develop and deliver transportation services, tapping the resources of the private sector to supplement those of the public sector to improve efficiency and effectiveness.

How transportation will evolve in terms of supply, demand, and character is as difficult to predict as the pattern of an NFL football game. However, key stakeholders among the various users and providers of transportation services can provide an indication of what they would like the surface transportation system to become in terms of the following characteristics:

- Stability of funding sources.

- Financial self-sufficiency during a transportation facility's service life based on the ability to reduce its costs and to charge transportation users and other beneficiaries

- Enhanced competition and choices for users that expand available transportation capacity.

- A broad portfolio of modal, service, project delivery, and financing choices that transportation leaders can apply to maximize the opportunities and resources available.

- Allocating the supply of transportation through value-based pricing to reduce over-use of available capacity and to provide additional funding to expand capacity.

- Significantly more investment in surface transportation based on adequate rates of return from user charges, or from social benefits funded by public subsidies.

- Reduced program costs from improved management, and from proper life-cycle stewardship of infrastructure facilities to maximize their service lives.

- Greater integration of transportation modes, including fund sharing between modes, public and private carriers, shippers, and logistics companies.

- Stronger focus on critical bottlenecks in surface transportation, especially within and between modes, and at such major transfer points as ocean shipping ports and rail/truck terminals.

- Enlisting private-sector carriers, logistics companies, and shippers in planning, funding, and financing services that are better able to meet their individual needs.

These elements of a sound transportation vision emphasize greater competition among providers, more customer choices, price-based rationalization of mobility demands, integration among modes and carriers, performance accountability by transportation providers, private and public cooperation and coordination in developing facilities and providing services, and customer-driven use of new technology to improve transportation quality. The result should be a more balanced, more inclusive, self-sustaining program. In other words, the right transportation strategy is one that anticipates and responds to the needs that customers are willing to pay for.

Strategic Initiatives

A sound vision requires that we undertake a series of strategic initiatives. These must include both short-term and long-term actions by transportation program sponsors and stakeholders. Such initiatives form the basis for the sixth driving question.

6. ***What do we need to do in the short-term and the long-term to move from our current situation to the shared vision of transportation stakeholders?***

Institutional Change

- Engage all stakeholders in defining current problems and developing a vision for the future shape of surface transportation in America.

- Develop policies and strategic plans that will support this vision and embrace all levels of government, private sector transportation providers, and transportation customers.

- Focus the federal government's transportation activities on clearly defined national interests that are constitutionally mandated federal responsibilities, including interstate and international commerce, and our domestic and international security.

- Consolidate the mode-specific surface transportation administrations within the Department of Transportation by combining FHWA and FTA into a single administration, and integrating their programs so block grants go to state and local governments in ways that transcend individual modes.

- Delegate to state and local governments most surface transportation program authority and responsibility for intercity and local roads, regional railroads, and public transit while the federal government maintains authority and responsibility only for transportation programs that have a clear national significance.

- Reduce modal and institutional fragmentation by expanding competition, customer choices, user pricing, beneficiary-based funding, public-private and public-public partnering, performance accountability, and technological innovations.

Funding and Financing Change

We need to promote and enhance opportunities for developing, testing, and implementing alternative funding sources while phasing out motor vehicle fuel taxes over the next 10 to 15 years. This does not mean we should discount the need to consider indexing and increasing the existing federal motor fuel tax to maintain the system at existing levels during the transition period. Such alternative sources can include:

- Direct user charges, including roadway tolls, vehicle mileage-based charges, and truck-only toll lanes, especially on limited access highways (including portions of the Interstate Highway System), and on other major highways in densely populated metropolitan regions that are subject to high levels of traffic congestion.

- Capturing the economic development benefits of enhanced accessibility through tax-increment financing, developer contributions of right-of-ways, and special tax assessment districts.

- State sales taxes or other local option taxes dedicated to funding surface transportation.

- Fund sharing among public and private stakeholders that have mutual interests in multi-modal projects.

- Sale of air rights, naming rights, and other alternative revenue sources.

Project Cost Change

Develop and institute strategies that reduce surface transportation costs by requiring life-cycle stewardship of plant and equipment to lower replacement frequency and costs.

- Use asset-management principles to preserve facilities at desired service standards, including greater emphasis on preventive maintenance to extend service lives.

- Modernize facility design and construction for longer years of service at lower life cycle costs, as detailed in the FHWA's Highways for Life program in SAFETEA-LU.

- Focus preservation efforts on facilities still in decent condition as it is more cost-effective to maintain them than entirely restore deteriorated ones.

- Replace those deteriorated facilities through one-time capital reconstruction or replacement programs to be included in preservation programs based on sound asset-management principles.

- Institute up-to-date operations management techniques, variable pricing to manage congestion, and technologies to increase the capacity of existing facilities, especially in the major metropolitan regions that generate the bulk of the nation's Gross Domestic Product.

- Require value engineering for all major capital projects to lower project costs.

- Provide more opportunities to use public-private partnerships to expedite financing and delivery of projects that can lower project costs by avoiding inflationary cost increases, applying best practices and new technology, and transferring more technical and other risks to the private sector.

- Use a portfolio approach by matching specific types of PPPs to individual projects based on their characteristics and the capabilities and needs of public sector sponsors and private sector providers. This model was successfully used in Hong Kong before it was reunified with China when a number of transportation infrastructure projects were developed, each using a different project delivery approach (DB, DBOM, DFOM, BTO, etc. – see Appendix B for definitions) based on the nature of each project and the interests and risk tolerance of the participating members.

- More cost-effective approaches in metropolitan regions by providing greater linkages between highway and transit programs. In the case of transit programs, greater consideration should be given to such concepts as:

- Converting HOV lanes to HOT lanes with the U.S. DOT counting them as fixed guide-way miles for purposes of allocating formula-based funds.
- Developing Bus Rapid Transit (BRT) on user-priced highway lanes (such as express toll-lanes) and giving BRT operators toll discounts (up to 100 percent) for using these lanes.
- Make express toll-lane projects eligible for federal New Starts funding as part of the National Initiative to Reduce Congestion program announced by Secretary Mineta on May 16, 2006 shortly before he left office.[29]

Program Change

Revamp the nation's surface transportation program by:

- Converting the current "Soviet-Style" highway program into a "Capitalist-Style" program by reducing the government control over the highway system.

- Recognizing that transportation is an interdependent, multi-modal system with multiple stakeholders and users that have differing needs and capabilities.

- Integrating multi-modal development, funding, and operations to allow facilities to leverage available project funding and advocacy.

- Encouraging communication, coordination, and cooperation between program stakeholders.

- Enhancing competition by involving the private sector in various forms of public-private partnerships to leverage public sector capabilities.

- Pricing highway travel consistent with the quality of services provided to motorists.

- Holding transportation providers accountable for performance, measured by meaningful procedures for reporting and evaluation.[30]

Organizational Change

Establish new organizational arrangements to improve current programs in state transportation agencies now threatened by funding and personnel shortages.

Some leading state transportation agencies are already initiating institutional and program changes to prepare the way for the evolution of the nation's transportation system into a more cost-effective and responsive model. These include state DOTs in Florida and Texas, which have created models that encourage private firms to apply the latest technologies and best business practices on behalf of public sponsors of transportation facilities, while holding private and public partners in these new arrangements accountable for the results over the long term. These two cases are described below.

***Florida's Turnpike* Enterprise** – The Governor and state legislature created this unique entity in 2002 as a "test-bed for change and innovation" within Florida's Department of Transportation (FDOT). It is able to apply creative methods and technologies to improve service and generate additional resources to undertake more programs and projects. As an alternative to the outright sale or lease of the Turnpike to the private sector, this new Enterprise reflects three principles: (1) providing a public service (i.e., transportation); (2) applying best business practices to improve cost-effectiveness; and (3) holding the Enterprise and its private-sector partners accountable to the public for program results. The following graphic shows the transformation of Florida's Turnpike into the Enterprise model.

ORGANIZATIONAL TRANSFORMATION OF FLORIDA'S TURNPIKE

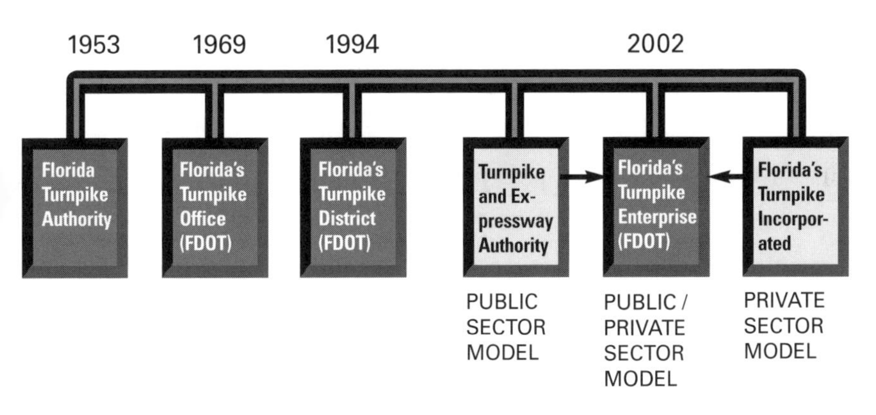

Source: From presentation by Jim Ely, Executive Director, Florida's Turnpike Enterprise, July 2002.

Under legislative authority, Florida's Secretary of Transportation can exempt the Enterprise from normal Florida DOT regulations, policies, and procedures so that it can experiment with innovative approaches to carry out its balanced mission.

Florida's Turnpike Enterprise Mission Statement

To help meet the State's growing transportation needs, ensuring value to customers, protecting investors, and managing the Turnpike System in a business-like manner

Florida's Turnpike Enterprise owns and operates a 449-mile system of tolled highways. It also collects tolls on an additional 125 miles of tolled highways and three tolled bridges that are owned or operated by Florida DOT. The Enterprise operates as a quasi-independent entity that reinvests all net cash flow back into the Florida Intrastate Highway System for upgrading, expanding, and building new toll facilities. More than 90 percent of its 4,600 staff members are employees of private firms that provide most of the Enterprise's line and administration functions under contract. The main exceptions are state police troopers assigned to the Enterprise and those holding its top management positions—all of whom remain state DOT employees.

By focusing on its public service mission and using best-business practices, the Turnpike Enterprise expects to generate over $10 billion in net proceeds during the next twenty years, all of which will be reinvested in tolled facilities within the Florida Intrastate Highway System. The Enterprise's current six-year capital improvement program is budgeted at $5.4 billion, which is expected to be funded primarily from tolls, supplemented by concession revenues and third-party contributions. During the next several years, the Enterprise will begin to convert to open-road tolling using advanced technology to eliminate tollbooths and collect tolls electronically or by mail.

Texas Department of Transportation - Under the Texas model, a wide variety of methods are used to promote the development of additional transportation capacity Texas residents and business firms will need during the next 50 years. This is best exemplified by the Trans Texas Corridor (TCC) program, which is intended to propel Texas ahead during the 21st century by developing a new, primarily self-funded multi-modal transportation network linking the state's major cities.

The 4,000-mile TTC network will consist of a series of interconnected corridors with toll highways for automobiles, separate toll lanes for trucks, and right-of-ways for freight, intercity passenger, and commuter rail lines as well as various utilities, as shown on page 162.

Laws passed by the state legislature during the past five years give the state government the ability to pursue innovative approaches for financing and developing infrastructure in an expedited manner, and provides a broad framework to promote public-private partnerships that supplement scarce public resources with private and local resources under several organizational arrangements:

Comprehensive Development Agreements (CDAs) establish a framework for comprehensive project planning, and for financing, building, operating and maintaining the resulting facilities through collaborative efforts between Texas DOT and private developers. These arrangements may involve the developer performing all or some of these functions on a project-by-project basis, or another development team producing

TRANS-TEXAS CORRIDOR CONCEPTUAL PLAN

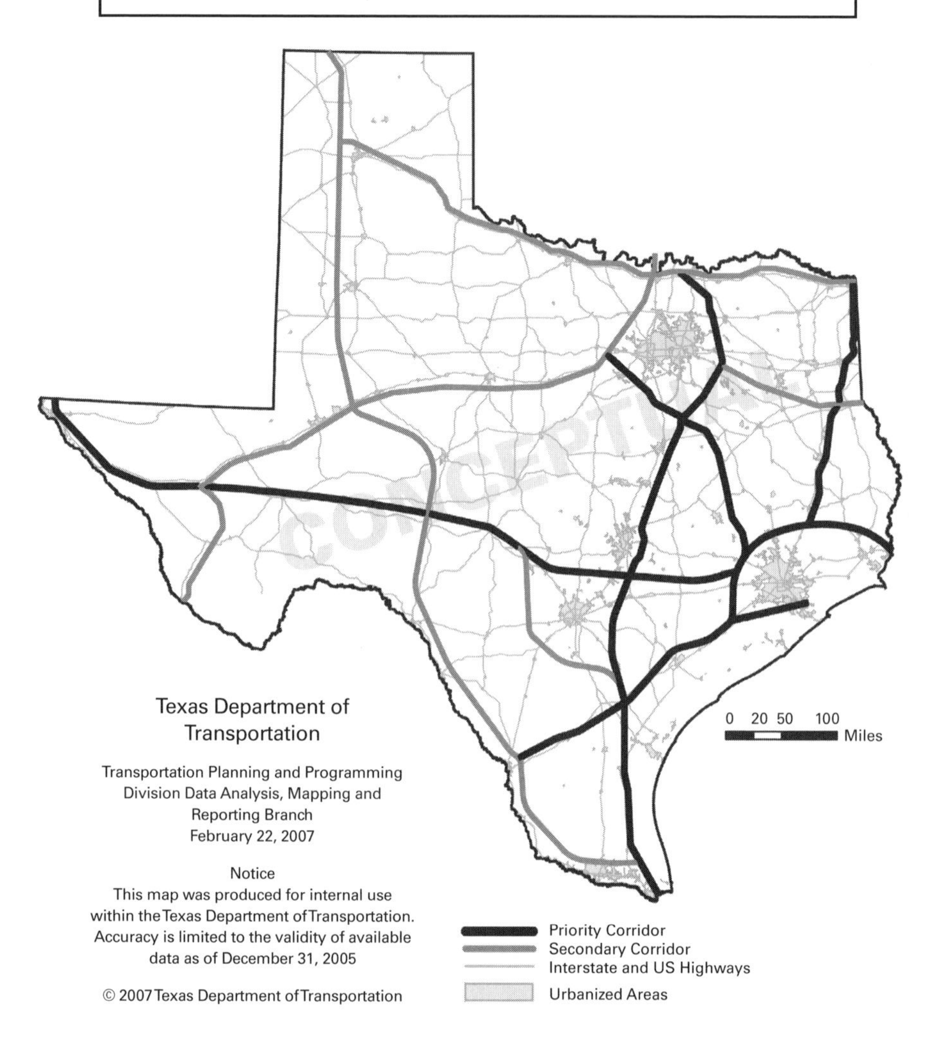

the facility, or Texas DOT itself doing the project. CDAs have let Texas DOT get around the lack of specific legal authority to use such innovative PPP approaches as Design/Build. In all cases, Texas DOT remains the public sponsor of PPP arrangements though its Turnpike Authority, with various private teams developing each project.

Regional Mobility Authorities (RMAs) are public authorities established by local jurisdictions to function independent of Texas DOT in the development and execution of PPPs, thereby significantly decentralizing the planning and delivery processes. Under this flexible legislation, Texas DOT, the Texas Turnpike Authority, and Regional Mobility Authorities accept solicited and unsolicited proposals for project PPPs. The legislation allows state and local authorities to approve the methodology used by private entities to set and raise toll rates, but not to set the rates themselves.

A variation of the Regional Mobility Authority has been proposed by this author and is described as follows:

Regional Mobility Corporations (RMCs) are public-private corporations established to apply innovative financing, project delivery, and preservation approaches to add to a region's stock of transportation infrastructure. Unlike RMAs, the board of directors include members from the public sector, like state and local government agencies, and the private sector, including project developers and others, like banks, large utilities, major shippers, and transportation/logistics companies. Through its private sector members, an RMC is like a commercial enterprise that can provide a more entrepreneurial approach while the government members ensure that the public interest is safeguarded and that there is public accountability.

As project sponsor, this quasi-private organization would have even broader access to capital financing sources than public sponsors for use on a regional, portfolio basis to fund reconstruction, modernization, expansion, and otherwise enhancing infrastructure assets. By its very nature, financing sources available to an RMC would include private equity from the corporation's shareholders, which might come from pension funds, insurance funds, and infrastructure funds specifically established to invest in transportation infrastructure. This would reduce the need for debt capital, thereby providing greater financing flexibility regarding the timing and relative use of equity and debt financing, which could enable RMCs to achieve lower overall costs of capital when compared to conventional revenue-bond debt used by most state-owned public authorities.

The private aspect of the RMCs allows them to expedite the use of new technologies and reap the benefits of improved system management, greater travel safety, and integrated traveler information.[31] These are prerequisites if the domestic and international financial markets are to become major players in supplementing scarce public funds. This will end today's over-reliance on the Transportation Innovative Financing Initiatives Act program (TIFIA) loans and municipal bond financing of toll roadways by introducing innovative financing tools and tapping new sources of financing like pension and insurance funds. These sources have vast amounts of capital seeking long-term investment opportunities with stable, risk-managed cash flows to support the necessary returns to their customers.

Underlying Principles

There are certain basic principles that should guide our strategy for a new vision for surface transportation that reflect the distinctive culture and character of the United States. This forms the basis for the seventh driving question:

7. ***What fundamental principles should be followed in developing and executing a new vision for surface transportation in America?***

Public Ownership of Roads, Bridges, and Tunnels

The legal title to right-of-ways should continue to be held by state or local governments. This ensures proper accountability to the public, due consideration for the public interest, and proper concern for public safety, security, and emergency issues. It also facilitates acquisition of land that may be needed for transportation facilities, since only government has the right of eminent domain to take private property for public purposes.

One exception to this is when a private developer purchases land parcels, then proceeds to finance and develop the facility on either a build-transfer-operate (BTO) or build-operate-transfer (BOT) basis. In the BOT case, the developer retains title to the facility to operate and maintain for a specified period of years, then turns it over to the public sponsor in a condition that meets the standards set in the BOT contract.

Another exception is when government establishes a commercial corporation to own and operate the roadway network in a metropolitan region on a self-supporting basis by charging tolls on its limited-access highways. Government becomes one of the primary owners of this corporation by exchanging its roadways for equity shares.

Taking a Life-Cycle Approach

For many in the transportation community, the concept of the future extends no further than the next five or ten years. With six-year reauthorization cycles, one or two-year budget cycles, and four to six year elective office terms, the public sector has difficulty looking much beyond. The private sector may not be constrained by term limits or program timeframes, but publicly traded companies are subject to quarterly reporting and often face pressures from Wall Street to show positive results in the short-term, even at the expense of long-term results.

The fact is that transportation facilities generally have service lives of 20, 50, or even 100 years. So there is a serious disconnect between the long-term vision needed to provide proper stewardship of this infrastructure at lowest life-cycle costs and the pressure on public and private sector managers to show immediate results. Thus we need to find ways to ensure commitment to long-term, life-cycle infrastructure management.

One solution may be for the kind of government-sponsored corporations mentioned above to own and operate more transportation facilities. Private investors buying equity shares in these corporations will be attracted primarily by their long-term dividend flows, which depend on sound life-cycle asset management rather than rapid stock price appreciation. This might well balance the agenda of the government owners whose planning horizons are inevitably limited by short-term election cycles.

Pricing Scarce Capacity

Except for the domestic airline industry, which continues to lose more money than it's ever made, deregulation of commercial transportation has unleashed the creative capabilities of many successful transportation carriers. They've used aggressive pricing and more cost-effective operations to secure larger market shares and boost their profitability.

Deregulation has given customers more service choices and increased productivity such that it helped spur the nation's economic growth during the past 25 years. In the 1980s and 1990s, for instance, freight transportation deregulation helped to promote the just-in-time inventory concept, rail system rationalization, and the

North America Free Trade Agreement (NAFTA). While trucking firms have become more competitive and cost-effective since deregulation, the same cannot be said of the highway program itself. Indeed, traffic congestion is even beginning to reverse the gains that freight carriers made in the aftermath of deregulation. With the nation's highway program facing funding challenges, the time is ripe to consider ways to "deregulate" the nation's highway program. Pricing of highway access is one way to accomplish this.

Almost all goods and services used by the public are provided at prices intended to reflect their value to the customer, as well as to cover the full costs of providing those goods and services. The positive difference between value and cost is profit, while the negative difference is loss. The greater the public's appetite for a particular service, the higher the price that can usually be charged and the amount of profit that can be earned. Indeed, pricing is used to ration the allocation of such basic necessities as water, food, fuel, and electricity.

Water is an especially relevant example of pricing basic commodities. In the mid-20th century, water was provided to homes at no direct cost to the user since the water department was a city or county department funded by general tax revenues. The consumer didn't need to conserve water since his level of use was not related to cost, which was buried in his annual property tax bill. As a result, consumption outgrew the capacity of the municipal water systems and major expansions were needed, which significantly increased the local property tax rate.

The result was that water supply and sewage treatment functions were turned into public utilities with a separate enterprise fund so they wouldn't have to depend on general tax revenues. To replace these lost revenues, water and sewer utilities priced water use and then for sewer service based on the amount of water consumed.

Eventually water and sewer rates per gallon consumed were adjusted to influence seasonal demand. With higher rates in the summer when more water was consumed and supplies became more limited due to less rain, and lower rates in the winter when consumption per household was less and precipitation provided more ample supplies. This reduced demand by encouraging consumers to conserve when rates were at their highest.

An interesting sidelight is the development of "designer" waters, such as Perrier, plain bottled water, and various bottled flavored waters. These are all much more expensive than water from the tap, where many firms actually fill their bottles. This is a consequence of artfully manipulated customer choice, as well as concerns in some areas about the quality of water produced by municipal water utilities.

The point is that water can be priced so that consumption is rationed, capacity requirements are reduced, improved technology is used for treatment and supply, and higher quality substitutes are encouraged. Since water is one of the basic requirements needed to sustain human life, its compatibility with market pricing suggests that the same compatibility applies to other essential goods and services, like access to the nation's roadway systems.

Pricing already rations the demand for such transportation services as parking, transit travel, air travel, rail-passenger travel, and goods movement. In the case of transit and intercity passenger rail, user prices are typically set below full costs to account for the social benefit to users and communities dependent on these services for accessibility and mobility. On transit systems, as on many toll roads, the user perceives a direct relationship between the price charged and the cost of use when paying the fare or toll. But since payment at the time of use indicates that transit and toll facilities are priced, toll-free highways are perceived to be free, like public parks.

Access to the nation's highways is one of the few basic services provided to the public that is not directly priced to reflect the quality of service or the quantity of use. One of the greatest challenges facing the highway community is how to move from this un-priced "public park" arrangement to market-based pricing. So, let's look for guidance to other sectors of the economy that have made the same transition, like cable and satellite television services, telephone services, and some Internet sites. These industries have provided greater choices of services to the public, greater integration of those services, lowered the costs for basic services while increasing costs for premium services, expedited use of new technology to expand and improve service quality, reliability, and content, and instituted differentiated prices based on time of day and day of week, to encourage greater use during off-peak periods. In the case of telephone and cell phone use, a greater leveling of demand across the day, has resulted in more efficient use of available capacity, which has reduced the need for capital expansion just to meet peak period demand.

Results from other capital-intensive industries demonstrate that when certain free-market requirements are met:

- Competition can generate improved performance, accountability, and innovation in the delivery of goods and services.
- Pricing can define the value that the customer places on the goods and services being offered, cover the cost of innovations and better services, and ration demand.
- Choices allow users to retain their traditional service and pricing plans, or to access higher-value services at higher costs if they wish.
- Linking the service provider and customer through pricing

mechanisms promotes responsiveness by the service provider, continued innovation to develop and offer new and better services more cost-effectively, and a commitment to provide the level of capacity and service quality that the public is willing to pay for, the most meaningful measure of customer demand.

User, Beneficiary Pay

In effect, to use the nation's highways, consumers are charged federal, state, and local taxes on the sale of petroleum-based motor vehicle fuels. These funds are augmented by state and local vehicle registration and licensing fees paid by automobile owners and drivers, plus general fund tax revenues. Trucks generally pay higher motor vehicle fuel taxes plus sales taxes on such items as tires.

Since fuel taxes are collected at the point of sale, they're not connected in the motorist's mind with travel on any particular roadway at any particular time. In the case of vehicle registration fees and licensing fees, these taxes are unrelated to how many miles the vehicle travels or the licensed individual drives.

Direct user charges are collected only on toll roadways, which make up only 3.3 percent of the National Highway System, and 6.4 percent of the Interstate portion of the system. Overall, toll facilities contribute only about 4.5 percent of the total U.S. highway program funds (FHWA, Highway Statistics 2004). Hence, highway travel in the U.S. is largely provided to users on a price-free basis. And as an un-priced commodity, highway travel continues to grow at increasing rates. This places even greater burdens on a transportation system that is barely able to support current levels of development in many of the nation's more urbanized communities.

Price-free commodities and services usually experience unconstrained consumption that eventually overwhelms the capacity to provide decent services, especially when public budgets are limited. Without a pricing policy to help manage travel demand on the nation's most highly congested highways, congestion will continue to worsen and the funding gap will continue to grow.

To counter this trend, we need to recognize that highways cost money to build, operate, and maintain. Pricing can be an effective way to better ration the use of scarce highway capacity while providing added financial resources to add capacity to the system.

Government Oversight

Government has a strong role to play even when transportation is provided by the private sector. This role includes acting as contract sponsor and administrator, as well as guarding the public interest in publicly owned and publicly used transportation facilities. That role can be enhanced through its financial participation, and sharing in its revenue risks and returns.

At the same time, government has the responsibility for assuring transparency in the procurement of services provided by private-sector members in public-private partnership teams, and in maintaining private and public sector accountability for performance according to the terms of the PPP contract. PPPs are not an excuse for government to abdicate its responsibilities to ensure the most cost-effective delivery of transportation to users, indirect beneficiaries, and providers – all of whom are stakeholders in the process.

Institutional and Modal Fragmentation

There are various ways to provide greater integration and coordination of transportation services.

- **The One-System Approach:** This would integrate different modes through traffic management, cross-subsidies for inter-modal connections, and removing system bottlenecks that inhibit greater integration. But surface transportation is composed of too many private and public components for this to be practical on anything other than very small scale. Having government try to integrate everything would be more difficult than "herding cats."

- **Survival of the Fittest or Winner Takes All:** A more practical approach may be to recognize the common ground and inherent differences among various stakeholders, and then build on these commonalities and differences so that all of them can contribute to the solution.

  To devotees of Adam Smith, this would take the form of an "invisible hand" producing more efficient and effective transportation. The public sector would provide services that the private sector is unable to operate profitably, or where the social benefits are sufficiently important to justify the use of public funds. The danger is that given transportation's monopolistic tendencies, this could lead to a wave of mergers between private transportation providers until only a few giants remain and competition is greatly diminished. This will only result in a return to the kind of government regulation that the past has shown produces highly inefficient transportation.

- **Optimal Solutions from Negotiating Among Competing Stakeholders:** Building on the concept of common ground and self-interest, another way to build better integration is for all stakeholders to participate in negotiations that recognize their respective interests and capabilities.

  Devotees of Dr. John Nash, Jr. would suggest applying "Equilibrium Theory." Nash argues that optimal results from negotiations among competing groups occur when all groups cooperate in the bargaining process, recognize the relative advantage of each group, and agree to allocate the benefits from solutions among groups according to their relative contribution to the solution.

  Equilibrium Theory has been the basis for corporate negotiations and international agreements for the past 50 years. When applied to transportation infrastructure with its many diverse stakeholders, it offers a proven way to bring the parties together early in the negotiating process to determine the relative position of each stakeholder and their willingness and ability to contribute to the solution.

- **Bridging the Differences between Various Modes:** The transportation system is fragmented by mode, ownership, technology, funding sources, administrative agencies and aid programs. But forced amalgamation is not the answer. Instead, we must seek out areas of common interest that can draw providers together and integrate the respective resources of stakeholders, while retaining the core features of each stakeholder group that enable it to do what it does best.

This should involve all levels of government as well as corporations that sponsor or depend on efficient transportation. What we need is a framework where all parties can come together to negotiate strategies, programs, and projects that serve their common interests.

This process begins by understanding what is to be optimized – whether that's lane-miles constructed, travel time reduced, noxious emissions reduced, or economic development goals achieved. This brings us back to the basic question of what are we seeking to achieve from the nation's surface transportation system in the 21st century?

Emerging Policy and Program Opportunities

Several initiatives, many of them quite recent, have been undertaken to address some of the challenges posed by current transportation programs, like funding, modal integration, rules and regulations, and institutional arrangements. This brings us to our eighth driving question:

8. *What policy, program, or process changes already underway would support the concepts contained in the proposed new vision for surface transportation in America?*

New Federalism: Devolution of Federal Role and Responsibilities

The U.S. Department of Transportation's actions and budget reflect a continuing shift of transportation program administration and funding responsibility to state and local governments. In shifting funding responsibilities to lower levels of government, the White House recognizes that in the future the federal government will have fewer program or project mandates and restrictive regulations.

The federal government's sponsorship of demonstration programs or pilot projects suggests that it is more focused on safety and congestion relief issues. It is also encouraging the states to make more use of PPPs to supplement scarce public funds, and foster innovative approaches to project development and delivery, and creative ways to generate the funding needed to preserve and develop infrastructure in an environmentally sound manner.

But this shift also implies that it is the obligation of state and local governments to make up for declining funds from the federal government. That means they have greater responsibility for funding and financing transportation projects across the modes, and must make more use of private resources to supplement scarce public financial and staff resources to:

- Provide preliminary concept development and planning support.
- Procure project and service delivery contracts, including PPP contracts.
- Develop program and project budgets.
- Set policy and service standards.
- Perform quality assurance.

- Hold contractors and concessionaires accountable for complying with contracts terms.

Increase Funding, Delivery, and Management Flexibility

The last three Congressional reauthorizations of federal transportation programs, as well as some intervening legislation, have provided state and local transportation agencies additional means to answer transportation resource challenges. Both the Intermodal Surface Transportation Efficiency Act (ISTEA) and the Transportation Equity Act (TEA-21) recognized the need to consider alternative financing and project delivery approaches in order to respond to rising concerns over the long-term financial viability of the Federal Transportation Trust Fund. The most recent reauthorization (SAFETEA-LU) included modest expansions of these initiatives, including the following:

- **The Interstate Tolling Program** – allows as many as three currently non-tolled interstate facilities to be tolled.

- **Private Activity Bonds** – provides up to $15 billion in tax-exempt financing to private-sector firms that make investments in highways and inter-modal facilities.

- **Promotion of Public-Private Partnerships** – involves special experimental programs to enable state transportation agencies to use innovative planning, financing, contracting, right-of-way acquisition, and environmental clearance consistent with NEPA that enhance the attractiveness of projects to private-sector partners.

- **Amendments to TIFIA** – authorize credit enhancement and loan assistance to private operators and expand eligible projects under the Transportation Innovative Financing Initiatives Act program.

- **Special Promotional Programs** – include pilot and demonstration programs to encourage facilities planning, pricing, and programming, like the National Strategy to Reduce Congestion on America's Transportation Network, the Value Pricing Program, Corridors of the Future, and Highways for Life.

The Charms of Public-Private Partnerships

Partnerships between state agencies and private firms offer a wide variety of options for project financing, delivery, operations, maintenance, and preservation. They involve differing levels of participation by public- and private-sector partners, depending on what the public agency is seeking and what the private firm is willing to provide.

The FHWA has defined PPPs as follows:

> *"A public-private partnership is a contractual agreement formed between public and private sector partners, which allow more private sector participation than is traditional. The agreements usually involve a government agency contracting with a private company to renovate, construct, operate, maintain, and/or manage a facility or system. While the public sector usually retains ownership in the facility or system, the private party will be given*

> *additional decision rights in determining how the project or task will be completed."*[32]

There is strong support from U.S. DOT leadership for the use of PPPs, a sentiment best expressed by current Secretary of Transportation Mary Peters when she was still FHWA Administrator:

> *"I want to be clear about where the Bush Administration stands, where U.S. DOT and Secretary Mineta stand, and where FHWA stands. We are for public-private partnerships. We support them. We want to make them easier, much easier to do.... Despite notable successes... public private partnerships are still viewed by many in transportation as unique and fraught with legal, financial, and administrative hurdles. Abundant experience in the use of PPPs in other areas, and the growing experience in transportation, illustrate that these hurdles can be overcome. We can lower costs and speed project completion. In a time of funding shortages at all levels of government, it is particularly important that we look to opportunities for the private sector to participate in funding transportation infrastructure improvements."*[33]

PPPs come in various forms, depending on the extent to which the private or public sector partners assume the roles, responsibilities, risks, and returns associated with the projects. Shifting project cost, schedule, and quality risks to the private sector are key reasons for public transportation agencies to consider entering into PPP arrangements, especially for large-scale and complex projects. Many U.S. DOT initiatives encourage states to pass legislation permitting the use of PPPs for surface transportation projects, including highway and transit New Starts capital projects.

PPPs range from contract maintenance and design-build arrangements to concession leases and asset sales (see Appendix B). The graphic below shows the relationship between different types of PPPs, and the degree of public versus private responsibilities and risks, listed in order of increasing private-sector involvement.

Relative Public and Private Roles for Different Types of PPPs

PUBLIC RESPONSIBILITY AND RISK	PPP APPROACHES	PRIVATE RESPONSIBILITY AND RISK
LOW	Asset Sale	HIGH
	Concession	
	Joint Development Agreement (JDA)	
	Build-Own-Operate (BOO)	
	Build-Transfer-Operate (BTO)	
	Build-Operate-Transfer (BOT)	
	Design-Build-Finance-Operate (DBFO)	
	Design-Build-Operate-Maintain (DBOM)	
	Design-Build (DB)	
	Maintenance Contract	
	Design-Bid-Build	
HIGH	In-House Project Delivery	LOW

While the public sector is charged with providing transportation through roads and transit, it has a short attention span and limited perspectives regarding modes and timeframes, which may prevent them from generating the most appropriate resources to develop and operate the facilities that are built cost effectively. In most cases, PPPs are used because the public sector lacks adequate internal resources to expedite delivery of a needed transportation project or to service it in a cost-effective manner. Assigning the risks associated with project cost, schedules, and quality to the private sector can help address these issues through long-term financing, more cost-effective approaches to facility development, life-cycle asset management, and quicker adoption of the latest technologies.

Voter Support for Transportation Initiatives

The 2006 mid-term elections once again demonstrated that public referendums on transportation-related tax and bonding initiatives are more often supported when the economy is strong than during a recession. Amid a strong and expanding economy, 7 state ballot initiatives for transportation were approved in all 6 states where they appeared. Six of these initiatives increased or allocated more funding for transportation from a variety of sources, including:

- Sales taxes on motor vehicles (Minnesota and California).
- Government-backed bonds (California and Rhode Island).
- Higher proportion of motor vehicle fuel taxes dedicated to transportation (New Jersey).
- Proceeds from the sale of special license plates (Georgia).

Local transportation revenues were reduced only in Louisiana, where voters rejected the right of local governments to place an ad valorem tax on motor vehicles.[34]

Voters seem willing to approve various ways to increase funding for transportation projects involving highways and transit. On the other hand, elected federal and state officials have generally resisted efforts to increase motor vehicle fuel taxes for fear of voter backlash. Even with the change in Congressional leadership after the 2006 mid-term election, an increase in the federal motor fuel tax rate is not likely due to the continuing high cost of petroleum and the fear that a tax hike would paint the new Democrat-led Congress as a "tax-and-spend" crowd.

Major Challenges

To achieve a sound vision for transportation in America, policy-makers, program decision-makers, and key stakeholders need to understand, anticipate, and overcome key challenges to changing the status quo. This is addressed in the ninth driving question:

> 9. *What is likely to hold us back and what can stakeholders and sponsors do to overcome these barriers?*

The obvious answers include:

- Institutional inertia in federal, state, and local governments and among traditional private sector stakeholders who resist efforts to change or reinvent the nation's surface transportation program.

- The tendency to continue the existing program through Congressional reauthorizations rather than developing a more flexible, more equitable, more self-sufficient and longer lasting, program – in other words, scrapping the existing reauthorization process and starting over with a clean slate.

- Failure to open the surface transportation program to free-market forces that invite more competition, accountability, and better life-cycle management.

- Reluctance by private sector transportation providers and users to become committed to the vision of transportation in America and the requirements needed to achieve it.

- Constantly overstating funding requirements, underestimating ways to reduce program costs through better management of existing infrastructure.

- Failing to recognize the impact on transportation of demographic changes, and ignoring the possibilities for alternative work location choices that incorporate options like telecommuting.

Without understanding where we are, where we want to be, and the consequences of not changing the status quo, we lack adequate incentives to move forward. If we have not agreed on a master vision, toward which our efforts are directed, virtually any set of strategies will appear to be valid. That is why the space program lost public enthusiasm, political support, and adequate funding after the Apollo program ended because the Shuttle program was seen as a mission without a vision or a destination.

To remedy this, NASA has attempted to develop a new vision for America's space program, dubbed "Earth to Moon to Mars and Beyond," in which the Shuttle Program is ultimately replaced by a more cost-effective mission focused on specific destination-oriented targets with heavy involvement and investment by the private sector and the international community. If this works, it can lead to a more sustainable and expanding space exploration program, rather than the existing "mission to nowhere."

The nation's transportation program requires a similar overhaul. One that focuses on the issues, opportunities, and challenges that are most critical to the nation's economic vitality. These include the realities of an expanding global economy, shifting trading alliances, new technologies, changing demographics, and the evolving mobility needs of transportation stakeholders.

Conclusions

What can the strategic failure of the Imperial Japanese Navy in planning the Pearl Harbor attack teach us about not allowing business-as-usual traditions to blind us about the right things to do when it comes to overhauling surface transportation in the United States?

It happens that the Imperial Navy's officially sanctioned model for everything it thought and did was the British Royal Navy. But standard histories of the Royal Navy emphasize its victories in spectacular naval battles like Trafalgar during which RN warships attacked and destroyed opposing warships. Thus, the Imperial Navy's thinking inevitably focused on attacking the U.S. Pacific Fleet's battleships while they were moored at Pearl Harbor. Lost in the shuffle was any serious consideration of trying to cripple Pearl Harbor's ability to function as a forward naval base.

So it was that, in one of history's finest displays of brilliant tactical management, 6 of the world's best aircraft carriers under the command of Vice-Admiral Chuichi Nagumo furtively approached the Hawaiian Islands from the north just before dawn that fateful

Sunday, launched their planes into the rising sun, caught the U.S. Pacific Fleet at Pearl Harbor with its pants down and under Commander Mitsuo Fuchida, wrought havoc in spectacular fashion. On paper at least, this rivaled the Royal Navy's triumph at Trafalgar, the Imperial Navy's benchmark of success.

But so what?

The American battleships at Pearl Harbor were slow-moving antiques from the World War I era. As we've seen, the U.S. Navy already had two brand-new battleships in its Atlantic Fleet that could run rings around them. And it was building 8 more that were even better.

More importantly, the Pacific Fleet's 3 aircraft carriers weren't at Pearl Harbor, neither were the 3 carriers in the Atlantic. Meanwhile, American shipyards were already building 10 modern carriers whose planes would devastate Imperial Navy forces in the great air/sea battles of the Philippine Sea, and Leyte Gulf later in the Pacific War. Moreover, the Air Force program was moving quickly to produce the B-29 bombers that would burn down 66 Japanese cities and drop nuclear bombs on Hiroshima and Nagasaki.

Most critical of all, as the sun set on December 7 while the U.S. Navy gathered the bodies of its 2,117 sailors and Marines slain in the day's combat, Pearl Harbor's all-important fuel storage and ship repair facilities remained untouched by Japanese bombs. Allowing it to continue serving as a forward base for American naval power in the Pacific. So in reality, December 7 marked the sunset of Japan's extravagant ambitions to dominate Asia. Admiral Yamamoto and the Imperial Navy's other tradition-bound leaders chose the wrong targets at Pearl Harbor.

The dictates of tradition are usually the worst guides to follow when it comes to doing anything really important. After all, if they've survived long enough to be venerated as tradition, they're probably obsolete. The world of surface transportation in the United States is beset by a host of traditions that have helped to produce the problems we face today. So we must free ourselves of them if we're ever to come up with a truly effective vision for what the shape of transportation should look like in the coming years.

The tenth question plays such a large role in transportation's future that it takes up the next chapter: How can new and emerging technologies help address the fiscal, congestion, and safety challenges of achieving the new vision for transportation in America?

Chapter 6: Adopting Technology

New technology can either be the most exciting thing since stud poker or a damn nuisance that costs too much money. Which one depends on how savvy we are in managing its transition from the idea stage to the marketplace. This is especially true in transportation, where we confront a surge of new technology coming on line or looming just over the horizon.

Here's a success story about how this transition worked for one technology that became hugely popular.

Rise of the Personal Computer

Today, the word *computer* calls up visions of millions of user-friendly little boxes on office desks, in homes of every description, on the laps of travelers sitting in airport boarding lounges or even on sunny beaches. Being used with unselfconscious aplomb by school children and their grandparents. By Gucci-suited investment bankers planning their next multi-billion dollar M&A deal. By soccer moms trying to keep their over-programmed schedules straight. By secretaries struggling to turn the latest ramblings of their bosses into something readable. By starving writers hoping to create the next great American novel.

But things were very different a generation ago. In those days, *computer* meant a multi-million dollar collection of large electronic boxes with blinking lights. Busily processing payrolls or accounts receivable for a large corporation in a climate-controlled room. The average American never even saw a computer except in science-fiction movies (where it often went crazy and killed people, or tried to seduce the heroine).

If you were an engineer or financial analyst working for a corporation large enough to have its own computer, you might wonder if it could help you save time solving numbers-oriented problems. In which case, you had to approach the techno-speaking priesthood who presided over it. Explain what you needed in the politest terms you could muster. Watch the priests listen impatiently. Then hear them tell you in sneering tones what they were prepared to give you. Which was usually a far cry from what you needed.

So you gave up and returned to your log-log duplex decitrig slide rule. Or to the multi-function mechanical calculator clattering away on your desk. Or possibly you learned to write special-purpose programs for yourself in FORTRAN, which the priesthood might allow you to run on the computer.

But this often meant that you had to spend much of your time being a computer programmer. Which left you with too little time to actually work as an engineer or analyst with the results that the FORTRAN programs gave you.

How did the computer evolve from a Mainframe Monster of relatively limited utility into today's user-friendly personal tool that seems as handy as a pocket comb? The story's an interesting one and can teach us a great deal about how to effectively manage technology. In transportation or any other field.

Here are the highlights.

From Hobby Kits to Consumer Entertainment Products

Back in the early 1970s, several mail-order firms began selling kits like the Altair that enabled techno-geeks to cobble together small working models of digital computers.

Many of these hobbyists came from the world of Ham radio, so they knew how to solder wires together and read electrical schematics. But in order to make these "microcomputers" actually do anything more than blink their rows of lights in random patterns, they had to write binary computer programs in Machine Language. Which most Americans find more difficult to learn than Mandarin.

One of these hobbyists was Steve Wozniak, whose day job was working for Hewlett Packard designing electronic calculators. After building an Altair kit at home and seeing its limitations, he knew he could come up with something better. So with fellow hobbyist Steve Jobs, he designed and built the first Apple microcomputer in 1976 on a handy plywood board using inexpensive and readily available electronic components.

The Apple had two important features that raised it head and shoulders above kit-based models like the Altair:

- **You could plug a cheap electronic typewriter keyboard into the Apple's input port.** Since most people knew how to type, the keyboard gave them a much simpler way to enter programs and data.

- **You could plug the Apple's output port into a home television set.** This allowed the Apple to display results on a full TV screen in letters and numbers rather than just blinking lights.

Wozniak and Jobs demonstrated the original Apple at an evening meeting of their local Homebrew Computer Club, where it created a sensation. In fact, the owner of a neighborhood consumer electronics store was so impressed that he offered to carry ready-to-run Apples for sale to his customers.

During the year that followed, the store sold about 200 Apples at a price of $666 and the two Steves realized that they had the makings of a profitable small business on their hands. So in 1977, they incorporated Apple Computer and got serious about becoming successful in the home computer business.

To boost their chances, Wozniak completely redesigned the Apple to give it more computing oomph, plus improved features like its own color TV monitor and one of the then-new miniature floppy disk drives that could store and run various computer programs and data. Now you could actually play simple arcade games like Pong on it.

This redesign was called the Apple II, sold for $1298, and proved to be very popular. Especially after Harvard dropout and computer programmer Bill Gates adapted a programming language called BASIC to run on the Apple II. BASIC enabled serious users to write their own programs in English phrases and simple algebra rather than in hard-to-learn Machine Language.

The popularity of the Apple II spawned a host of imitators among new and existing companies that saw attractive profit potential in what was becoming the "home computer industry." One of the most important was the Tandy Corporation, which marketed its TRS-80 system (popularly known as the "Trash-80") through its nationwide chain of Radio Shack stores. Tandy's national retail distribution, competitive pricing, and constant upgrades to the TRS-80 line quickly enabled it to become the new industry's sales leader. So the microcomputer (still called the "home computer") had arrived as a hot new consumer entertainment product.

VisiCalc Opens an Important Door

The 1979 release of the VisiCalc spreadsheet program changed everything. Virtually overnight, it enabled home computers like the Apple II to become serious business and engineering tools. Not just fun-to-use personal entertainment products like TV sets or stereos.

Accountants, financial analysts, and engineers had long used hand-drawn spreadsheets (rows and columns of inter-related numbers) to evaluate quantitative data. But preparing spreadsheets by hand could be a real pain. A few mainframe computer spreadsheet packages were available, but they were clumsy and hard to use.

In 1978, Harvard Business School student Dan Bricklin conceived VisiCalc as a way to end the tedium of preparing financial spreadsheets by hand for case studies in his MBA classes. He teamed up with computer programmer Bob Frankston and computer magazine editor Dan Fylstra to develop VisiCalc as stand-alone software to run on the Apple II, the Tandy TRS-80, and other home computers. It went on sale in 1979 and became an immediate success.

More importantly, it caused many numbers-oriented types in the corporate world to run out and buy home computers for their offices just so they could use VisiCalc for their work. Like projecting next quarter's financial results. Or analyzing the daily patterns of stock prices. Or solving engineering problems faster and more accurately than by using slide rules. So for the first time, computer purchases were software-driven rather than hardware-driven. This became a key marketing principle for the home computer industry.

The popularity of VisiCalc (and improved clones like SuperCalc and MultiPlan) among professional number-crunchers led to home computers becoming nearly as common in many offices as copying machines.

Enter Big Blue

In 1980, IBM woke up to the fact that home computers had become a thriving new industry and couldn't be ignored.

Quite candidly, top management didn't see how any serious money could be made in this market. But how could the world's largest computer manufacturer not be a dominant player in anything that had *computer* stamped on it? Especially if this could be done quickly and on the cheap. Not to mention quietly (in case the results turned out to be embarrassing).

So IBM put a small design team led by Don Estridge to work in Florida, outside the clutches of the corporation's formal (and highly bureaucratic) design process. In about a year, they came up with the first IBM-PC. With PC standing for "Personal Computer", which soon became the new generic name for all microcomputers. It went on sale in 1981.

- To save time and money, Estridge's team used off-the-shelf components that were widely available from a number of electronic parts manufacturers. (Quite a difference from IBM's standard practice of using only parts that it designed and manufactured itself.)

- They designed the PC around an "open architecture" approach to make it easy for other companies to develop compatible hardware add-ons and software. A prime example was Mitch Kapor's legendary Lotus 1-2-3 spreadsheet software, which was so good that it became the standard for all PCs and sent VisiCalc and its clones to early graves.

- They contracted with Bill Gates to have his fledgling Microsoft company write new software for the PC's operating system, which they built into the PC (and its retail price) under the name "PC-DOS."

- They arranged to have Sears Roebuck and the national Computerland store chain handle retail sales.

By any measure, the IBM-PC was a revolutionary product and its impact was enormous.

- The international clout of IBM's name made personal computers truly respectable. Especially in the corporate-office market, where buying IBM-PCs and its applications software like Lotus 1-2-3 became the first practical way for users to bypass the long-established tyranny of mainframe computers and their less-than-cooperative priesthoods. For in those days, virtually everyone subscribed to the carefully cultivated mantra that "nobody ever got fired for buying IBM." This enabled IBM to quickly dominate the personal computer industry. Which most people considered only natural and even inevitable (but lasted only a short time).

- On the flip side, the IBM-PC's open architecture and use of off-the-shelf parts made it easy for ambitious young companies like Compaq and Dell to produce cheaper "PC compatibles" that could run any software written for the premium-priced IBM. In fact, not only were these clones cheaper. They were often better performers. This combination of lower price and better performance attracted customers in growing numbers. To the point where IBM eventually lost its quasi-monopoly in the personal computer industry, became a fast-fading minor player during the 1990s, and finally left the business entirely by selling out to a Chinese company in 2000. But all the while, its original concept of the personal computer as a practical tool for homes and offices sailed on to ever-greater success. Eventually surpassing automobiles and TV sets in unit sales throughout the world.

- IBM's arrangement with Bill Gates to write the PC-DOS operating system for its original PC left him free to sell copies of the software to other customers under the name MS-DOS. This was a major factor in assuring meaningful compatibility with the IBM-PC for the clones produced by other manufacturers. It also became the whole basis for Microsoft's growth into one of the world's richest and most important corporations. Thus did a small fledgling software maker rather than a huge traditional hardware maker become the dominant force in the personal computer industry.

Word Processing for the Masses

The arrival in the 1980s of much-improved word-processing software, plus high-quality laser and ink-jet printers, enabled the IBM-PC and its clones to replace the traditional typewriter in offices and homes. This may be the most important reason why personal computers became so common, since most of them are used for word processing most of the time.

Looking back, it seems clear that the main advantage of the traditional mechanical typewriter was that its printed output was easy to read and fairly standardized. In law firms, advertising agencies, and other kinds of office-based operations where lots of letters, memos, and reports were the norm, this became a productivity issue.

But the traditional typewriter had many productivity shortcomings as well. If you accidentally made a typo or misspelled a word, you had to spend time making corrections by fussing with sloppy little bottles of whiteout fluid or awkward erasing tapes. And the corrections still showed. If you wanted to move a phrase or sentence to another part of the document where it seemed to read better, you had to re-type an entire page (sometimes two or more pages). Ditto if you wanted to add or delete a paragraph or two. All this took time. And more time increased the cost per document.

Inevitably, the proliferation of mainframe computers in large corporations during the 1960s sparked the desire to "semi-automate" the work of office typists to achieve greater productivity. This led to the development of word-processing software that could run on mainframes. And connecting mainframes to remote terminals that had electronic keyboards and TV screens.

Now you could type a letter or memo directly on the terminal's screen. Correct typos on the fly. Revise text on the screen. Save the document electronically and recall it later. And when the document was perfect, print it out in high-quality form on an electric typewriter connected to the mainframe.

All of which was a great improvement. But only if you worked for a company large enough and rich enough to have its own mainframe. And if typists could master the arcane terminology needed to make the system work. And if the mainframe wasn't too busy processing the bi-weekly payroll. And if the mainframe's priesthood didn't abruptly decide to shut it down for "maintenance" at the worst possible time (in accordance with the immutable mainframe law about "Murphy being an optimist"). In short, mainframe word processing was a step forward. But by no means the final step.

During the 1970s, many people thought the final step had been taken with dedicated word-processing systems like those produced by Wang Laboratories. They connected their remote terminals to comparatively inexpensive minicomputers that didn't require arrogant priesthoods to operate. And their software was more user-friendly.

But "comparatively inexpensive" still didn't make these dedicated systems cost-competitive with even the highest-end IBM Selectric typewriter. So systems like the Wang were still limited to fairly large office complexes. Most doctors' offices, law firms, and other small businesses had to continue using stand-alone typewriters.

Meanwhile, some surprisingly good word-processing software like the early versions of Wordstar was becoming available in the late 1970s for the Apple II, Tandy's TRS-80, and other popular home computers. The big hang-up was that the printers available for them were mostly dot-matrix machines whose geeky-looking print style and fan-fold paper wasn't considered sufficiently professional-looking for most offices.

All this changed shortly after the debut of the IBM-PC. Low-priced laser printers and (later) ink-jet printers became available for personal computers. They could print out letters on regular office stationery and reports on plain-copy machine paper. And their high print quality was indistinguishable from the most expensive electric typewriters. At the same time, the arrival of Word Perfect and Microsoft Word set new standards for user-friendliness and productivity-enhancing features in word processing software.

All this set the stage for the personal computer to be accepted as a logical replacement for the traditional typewriter in offices and homes. It was a stand-alone product about the same size and shape as an electric typewriter. Its keyboard had the same layout and was in more or less the same place. It was in the same price range but its software enabled it to do so much more, faster and more easily. Anyone who could use a conventional typewriter could easily learn to use a PC to type letters, memos, reports, books, tables, you name it.

So like a blossoming rose in springtime, the market among people who produced written material at work or at home opened wide to embrace the personal computer. This followed the same principle we saw earlier when professional number crunchers bought personal computers so they could use spreadsheet software – with their buying decisions being use-driven rather than hardware-driven.

The big difference was that the market of people who work with words is a great many times larger than the market of those who work with numbers. This helped turn personal computers into a giant industry during the 1980s and 90s.

A Summary of What Happened

Note the following interesting and significant progression of events:

- Companies like Apple, Tandy, and others turned the hobbyist's mail-order build-it-yourself microcomputer kit into a new home entertainment product like television sets and stereo systems that could be bought ready-to-use in retail stores.

- VisiCalc gave number crunchers easy-to-use spreadsheet software to run on the Apple II and other home computers. This moved them beyond the home and into the office as serious tools for accountants, financial analysts, and engineers. They bought the hardware because they wanted to use the software, not the other way around.

- IBM's entry into the home and office markets for microcomputers gave these products respectability, a catchy new generic name that quickly caught on, a wider range of useful software, and new standards for the whole industry. But its premium price and open architecture motivated Compaq and other companies to market "IBM-compatibles" that were often better and always cheaper, which helped to expand the customer base.

- The arrival of much improved word-processing software accompanied by high quality printers enabled personal computers to replace the traditional typewriter. First in offices, then in homes. In a comparatively few years, word processing became the primary use for the overwhelming majority of personal computers in service. Another case of people buying the hardware because they wanted to use the software. But able to penetrate a much larger customer base than just number crunchers.

Where Was the Government in All This?

Nowhere.

It didn't even realize what was happening. There were no government mandates to do this or that. No government-imposed "standards." No government seed money to help the fledgling personal-computer industry grow. No attempts by government to pick winners. Nothing.

Instead, the whole process was left to classic entrepreneurial capitalism guided by its so-called Invisible Hand.

Bright young technical types would get ideas for new kinds of personal-computer hardware or software. In a blaze of enthusiasm, they'd work out the details and cobble together some sort of prototype. Then go out seeking capital to turn their ideas into going businesses that would make them rich and famous. Hitting up relatives, friends, people they knew who ran retail chains that could sell their products, even (if they had the right contacts) professional venture capitalists, who were supposed to have an appetite for this sort of thing.

Most of these technical types never succeeded in raising a dime and their new ideas died in the womb. Among those who did succeed in raising start-up capital, most saw their little companies collapse inside of a year. Usually due to poor management (after all, these guys were creative technical types rather than trained managers), or dumb marketing mistakes (they weren't marketing pros either), or kindergarten financial controls (nor were they accountants). Their failures usually had nothing to do with how good their product ideas were.

The majority of those who survived their critical first year saw their companies limp along producing a return on invested capital that was generally lower than you could get from a risk-free savings account in a bank. But a precious few managed to sidestep enough pitfalls through some combination of skill and sheer luck to wind up making it big (like Apple Computer and Microsoft).

Most of the original capital invested in these personal computer start-ups was lost forever, which is what traditionally happens to start-up capital in any industry. Those who made it big might like to carry on about how they succeeded by standing on the shoulders of the giants who came before them. But it's probably more accurate to say that they succeeded by scaling the mountains of dead bodies left behind by those who failed.

Needless to say, critics of capitalism are appalled by the grand scale of waste that forms the bedrock of this entrepreneurial process. How, they agonize, can society tolerate it? Especially when we're all brought up to believe that waste of any kind (food, money, natural resources, etc.) is the eighth deadly sin.

A glib answer may be to stand on the shoulders of Gordon Gekko, the outsized villain of Oliver Stone's film *Wall Street*, and tell ourselves: "If Greed is good, then Waste is better."

After all, isn't that how the universe works? Ma Nature has a mad passion for the most extravagant kinds of waste. That's why she insists that a female frog lay thousands of eggs at a time. So that a few hundred may survive long enough to hatch into tadpoles. A few score of which may be lucky enough to avoid being eaten by greedy predators and mature into adult frogs.

If waste on such a scale is good enough for Ma Nature, who are we to argue? (Never mind how our mothers scolded us as kids to "think of the starving children in Africa" whenever we wasted food. Our mothers were obviously better people than Ma Nature. But that's another issue.)

A more philosophical answer may be to imagine all investors in a start-up industry as a single venture capitalist. Someone who's faced with a multitude of fledgling companies banging on his door for start-up capital. If he's really as savvy as he wants others to think, he knows there's no reliable way to pick winners because the whole world is a crap-shoot. So he invests equal amounts of capital in each opportunity and sits back to await the results.

Again, most of his capital is lost because most of these companies go under. Some survive long enough to pay back their capital, with interest that's less than the venture capitalist could earn by investing in risk-free Treasury bills. But a few may turn out to be Microsoft's. In which case, the venture capitalist earns a return large enough to cover all his losses with enough left over to make him look like an investor superstar.

In which case, the critic of capitalism may ask, why can't government be that lone investor supplying start-up capital with our tax dollars?

Not likely in the U.S. Something like that only happens in the new capitalist paradise of China, where it's become part of a concept known by the politically correct term "Socialism with Chinese characteristics" (don't wince, Chairman Mao).

Well then, our persistent critic may continue, why can't government offer guarantees to all investors providing high-risk start-up capital? If a start-up fails, the investor automatically gets his money back. We taxpayers share the loss, just as we share the gain if the start-up turns out to be another Microsoft.

Again, not likely in the U.S. Too much like government buying the poems East Village poets can't sell to the *New Yorker*. We only do that with farmers (overlooking the fact that Elizabethan England is remembered more for its poets than its farmers). But farmers are savvy enough to give themselves political clout. And enough political clout can get you anything.

But how can we expect investors to keep on supplying essential start-up capital if they're faced by the likelihood of such losses, our critic presses on (sweating visibly now)?

This question has two answers.

One is that the world is awash with more capital than it can find good investment opportunities for. If this capital is simply invested in risk-free Treasury bills (the practice of China and some Middle East oil countries), savers who supply capital will become discouraged and say, Why Bother? They'll either spend their savings on consumer goods. Or convert them into gold to hide under the proverbial mattress.

This answer relates directly to the second answer. Most investors are like people who bet on the horses. They mainly lose. In their hearts, they may even expect to lose. But whenever they get a few extra dollars together, they go to the local OTB parlor or their neighborhood bookie or the racetrack and bet on the horses. It's in their blood, so to speak. Like AIDS or heroin addiction. And where would the capitalist world be without them?

But there must be some alternative, our distraught critic insists (determined to give it one last shot). An alternative that avoids capitalism's appalling waste.

Sure there is. It's an alternative practiced in the former Soviet Union and other Leninist nations in cases where good payoffs were deemed to be critically important. Like developing the Soviet Union's first atomic bomb in the late 1940s.

Details of this story have emerged by slow degrees as Soviet archives from that era are gradually opened to Western scholars. Many key archives still remain closed, but the gist of the story appears to be more or less as follows:

As World War II in Europe was drawing to a close, the Soviet government knew that the United States was developing atomic bombs. So it had to develop its own as quickly as possible to keep pace with the U.S. Therefore, Stalin appointed his close colleague Lavrenti Beria to run this "Problem Number One" program (as the Soviets called the task of developing an atomic bomb).

Apart from having run the KGB successfully during the war, Beria had a reputation as a man who could get things done without a lot of excuses. One way he did this was through the time-honored practice of elbowing his way to the head of the line whenever possible. In this case, that meant using the KGB's carefully nurtured spy network in the U.S. to collect as much information as possible about what the Americans were doing and how. This produced a surprising amount of technical detail about the two separate approaches the U.S. followed to develop atomic bombs.

- **Approach Number One** produced the Hiroshima bomb (called "Little Boy"). Mechanically, it was simple enough to build. But it used an isotope of uranium that was extremely difficult to refine and required large amounts of scarce uranium ore to produce modest amounts of the isotope needed for each bomb.

- **Approach Number Two** produced the Nagasaki bomb (called "Fat Man"). It used an isotope called plutonium that was much easier to refine, didn't require nearly as much uranium ore, and was generally more efficient in the blast it produced. But its mechanicals were very complicated and posed some major engineering challenges.

So Beria faced some tough choices about which approach would work best for the Soviet Union. Or did he?

His solution was to call a meeting of the Soviet Union's best nuclear scientists, held at his third-floor office in the KGB's Lubyanka Prison building in downtown Moscow ("the tallest building in town," Alexander Solzhenitsyn is rumored to have quipped, "because you can see Siberia from its basement").

As theoretical physicists, these Soviet scientists were in every way the equal of their western counterparts. But most of their work had been done on paper because they'd never had access to proper laboratory facilities to test out their ideas. And they had plenty of ideas about the best way to build a bomb, which they debated eagerly in Beria's office.

Beria listened to the debate for about ten minutes. Then waved for quiet and pointed to two large stacks of file folders sitting on the floor next to his desk.

"These file folders contain all the technical information you need about the two ways the Americans built their bombs." he said. "And we know they worked. So let's save time and build our bomb their way."

The scientists gazed at the two stacks of file folders and swallowed nervously.

"I'm going to divide you guys into two teams." Beria went on. "Each team will be assigned one of the American approaches to use in building a bomb. And we'll see who wins. The winning team gets larger apartments, summer dachas on the Black Sea, lots of other new perks, and maybe even the Order of Lenin if I can swing it. The losing team gets sent to gulags. Okay?"

In August 1949, the Soviet Union tested its first atomic bomb. It was a refined version of the sophisticated Nagasaki bomb and, by all accounts, performed very well.

Details are still sketchy about what happened to the scientists. But the assumption is that most of them continued to work designing bombs, now that their nation was in the nuclear arms business.

Whoever said that Leninism never paid any attention to incentives?

A Nation Built on Technology

During the early years of the 20th century, such technological advances as electricity generation and distribution, incandescent light bulbs, wireless radio, and mass-produced automobiles radically changed the way America lived.

The years after World War II saw the average American's living standards increase significantly with the proliferation of such home appliances as television sets, clothes dryers, electric stoves, and automatic dishwashers. Each of these reduced housekeeping tasks sufficiently to enable more women to enter the work force.

The space program brought another surge in technology that filtered down to consumers. Computing and copying devices increased workplace productivity in the 1960s through the 1980s. During the 1990s, additional technology leaps further improved productivity by facilitating increased competition and value-based pricing in the telecommunications industry and further miniaturization of computing devices.

At the beginning of the 21st century, the stage is set to combine these advances with other emerging technologies to address the challenges facing American transportation.

This reality forms the basis for our final Driving Question:

- ***How can new technologies help address the fiscal, congestion, and safety challenges of achieving the new vision for surface transportation in America?***

Recent Technological Advances

Since the beginning of the Industrial Revolution, the pace of technological change has been accelerating. This can be seen in the features of late-model automobiles, as well as in devices now used by transportation agencies to help them manage the operations of roadway networks.

The influence of new technology on the quality of life and economic productivity is demonstrated by the rapid advances in telecommunications, document production, and computing technology during the past 25 years. This enabled new, small, more innovative firms like Microsoft and Apple to successfully compete with giants like IBM.

In addition to the personal computer, other important examples of innovative technologies that transformed our lives during the past 25 years include:

- Voice and data transmission capabilities via fiber optic cables instead of copper-wire lines.
- Printers, scanners, and copiers accessible to business firms and individuals.
- Portable hand-held cell phones for mobile communications of both voice and data.
- The 511 travel information systems being deployed in many states.
- GPS-based Blackberry and other personal communication devices.
- Bluetooth voice recognition technology to enable hands-free use of communications devices.
- The ubiquitous Internet, which has integrated many of the technological developments mentioned above into global communications and information-sharing networks.

In combination, these devices have revolutionized how business is conducted and where can employees work. Several technologies permit home-based telecommuting, which virtually eliminates the need for the daily commute to and from a downtown or suburban office location.

A pioneer in adopting new technology for highways is the toll-road industry. Many of its members are rapidly converting from manual, cash-based toll collection to cash-free electronic toll collection. The ultimate example of this is open-road tolling, which combines ETC with license place recognition technology to price vehicle use on toll roads without the need for tollbooths or the inconvenience of stopping to pay a toll.

Another pioneer is the trucking industry. Many firms have converted their fleets into high-tech rolling stock by equipping them with GPS-based tracking and security enhancements, trip routing and navigation aids, truck-to-truck and truck-to-dispatcher communications, and onboard vehicle diagnostics.

We've covered a fair amount of territory learning about the principles that can move technology from the idea stage to the marketplace. Now let's consider the specifics of new technology that can make transportation better and more cost-effective.

Key Features of New Technologies

The main challenge facing promoters of new technologies is to determine which of them the public really wants and how much it's willing to pay for them. The personal computer story showed us that the key features new technologies need to be successful include:[35]

- Interoperability.
- Open architecture.
- Compatibility with the technologies being replaced or augmented.
- Ease of implementation and use.
- User-friendliness for non-technical customers.
- Flexibility in adapting to the continuing emergence of still-newer technologies.
- The ability to combine a number of technologies to provide new service capabilities for current and new users.
- Technologies without applications have no market value.

Emerging and Future Transportation Technological Advances

These technologies will enable vehicles to operate more safety, reduce the possibility of accidents, automate certain functions that now require driver attention, provide real-time navigation information and guidance, and exchange information on vehicle and road conditions to permit more automated control of certain vehicle functions. One of the most important programs for encouraging and coordinating the development of new technology to improve driver safety and mobility is the Vehicle Infrastructure Integration (VII) initiative.

The VII initiative is currently being developed and has the potential to revolutionize transportation by creating an enabling communication infrastructure that can open up a wide range of safety and mobility applications. Dozens of potential applications have been identified, which can be broadly categorized within three areas: safety, mobility, and consumer and commercial applications.

For nearly 20 years, the U.S. DOT has envisioned an enabling communications network that permitted vehicle to infrastructure and vehicle to vehicle communication for a variety of vehicle safety and transportation operations. This vision became feasible when the Federal Communication Commission in October of 1999 allocated 75 MHz in the 5.9GHz band to the U.S. DOT.

That allocation has allowed the DOT to consider developing a viable communication link between vehicles and the roads that could accommodate safety and congestion applications. Also, the communication network known as VII will enable the deployment of a variety of applications that support private interests, including those of vehicle manufacturers. This network may have some interesting implications for market based pricing, toll roads and concession agreements, as we now know them. This area merits study.

The basic idea is that every car sold in the U.S. will have a communication medium (for example, a dedicated short-range communications radio) and a GPS unit in it and the nation's roadway network will be instrumented nationally to allow vehicles to communicate with roadside infrastructure. The deployment challenges are daunting. Simply consider, for example, that there are about 260 thousand signalized intersections in the U.S. Additionally, federal government wants to provide data not simply on freeways and the interstate network but on the arterial system as well. There are about 150,000 miles of arterials in the U.S. and some 50,000 miles of freeways and interstates.

The U.S. DOT has created a VII coalition consisting of all the relevant federal agencies as well as 10 state departments of transportation, the relevant trade associations and all major automobile manufacturers to evaluate what is the investment that is necessary to equip new vehicles and the roadway infrastructure with the new technologies and can the deployment be synchronized. The working groups have concluded that VII is technically feasible and have designed system architectures with multiple communication options. They still have outstanding work to complete on application development, privacy, data ownership, liability and business issues to resolve.

Some people have suggested that federal mandates be used to dictate combining various privately developed technologies falling under the umbrella of VII or ITS. Others prefer a market-driven approach to encourage adoptions of those technologies that respond best to public and commercial needs. There are lessons to be learned here from the personal computer industry and the development of the internet as suggested earlier.

VII evinces many of the characteristics of new technologies trying to gain market acceptance. For example, there have been many potential applications identified but no one know which ones are of interest to paying customers, be they the vehicle buying public or state transportation agencies. The "value propositions" therefore are still under development.

VII program is considering field tests that involve actual customers to demonstrate which technologies are most likely to produce meaningful benefits.[36] Examples of private-sector companies involved in piloting these new technologies include manufacturers of automobiles, trucks, and transit equipment, who are motivated by their desire to differentiate their products in order to attract more customers.[37]

Several auto manufacturers are already working intensively to bring these technologies to the market through research and development and pilot testing of prototype VII systems.

Here are three promising examples.

- In September 2006, the Nissan Motor Company announced a VII pilot project that will run from October 2006 to

March 2009 and involve about 10,000 drivers who subscribe to Nissan's telematics services. If successful, full commercialization of the system is expected in 2010.[38]

- In October 2006, BMW announced adoption of the DUST Network. This will provide real-time traffic information for 2007 model cars equipped with navigation systems, including dynamic routing and traffic flow projections.[39]

- Beginning in September 2006, the Road Charging Interoperability (RCI) project supported by the European Commission began working together with the CESARE III project that's supported by European association of toll road operators (ASECAP). The goal is to create a common interoperable Electronic Fee Collection (EFC) system for members of the European Union.[40]

Similar coordination efforts are beginning in the United States among key stakeholders like ITS-America, IBTTA, and the auto manufacturers through the VII program. Their goal is to address the lack of interoperability among proliferating toll collection systems in different parts of the nation (EZ-Pass in the Northeast and upper Midwest, SunPass in Florida, and similar systems in such states as Texas, Oklahoma, Kansas, and California).

Major Technology Challenges

Key challenges to successfully implementing new technologies in the transportation marketplace include:

- Public resistance to Big Brother mandates by government (market pull versus market push).

- Lack of perceived value and acceptance among the ultimate customers.

- Lack of standardization, compatibility, and interoperability among various technologies.

- Rapid obsolescence that reduces the profit potential of new technology.

Addressing these challenges will require prudent business decisions by private and public sector sponsors based on enhanced safety, improved mobility, and other features that travelers truly value. Having the competitively oriented automobile manufacturers spearheading VII program efforts is a positive sign that new technologies offering improve travel safety and mobility can gain traction with the public.

We're already seeing this kind of integration of enabling technologies in the trucking industry and the toll highway industry.

For several years, trucking firms have been equipping their truck cabs with sophisticated technologies, including GPS-based communication, navigation, and tracking equipment. The trucking and shipping industries has also begun to equip their trailers with sophisticated transponder devices to facilitate tracking, reduce theft, and ensure the integrity of security devices contained in the trailer.[41]

A number of toll road operators have converted from the traditional manual handling of cash at tollbooths to the more customer-friendly open road tolling process. Technology replaces the tollbooth and toll collector and eliminates stop-and-go lines of vehicles waiting to pay tolls.

Complete elimination of toll plazas and tollbooths is also planned by several toll operators in the U.S. This is based on the model provided by the 77 mile 407 Express Toll Route (ETR) north of Toronto in Canada, which pioneered this approach when it first opened in 1997.[42] This kind of technology facilitates the move to market-based pricing of highway use and enhances the potential for greater competition in financing, developing, and operating roadway systems.

Pace of Technological Change

As noted above, a major challenge for producers and consumers of this technology is the increasing pace of change. This can make investments in new technology highly risky if devices become obsolete before being able to generate an appropriate investment return.

Other challenges include lack of interoperability among technology produced by different manufacturers or sponsored by different agencies. Not to mention concern over individual privacy and how data produced by the VII network and technologically enabled automobiles will be used and stored. In Europe, the formation of the European Union provided the catalyst for efforts to integrate tolling systems across the continent to make road-charging systems fully interoperable and functionally seamless. This is similar to what the Euro has done for currency standardization in Europe.

Conclusions

The United States is never going to have the world's lowest labor costs. Or unlimited access to inexpensive raw materials. If we can't work cheaper, we've got to work smarter. Managing new technology properly is one of the ways we can work smarter to improve transportation.

Here's an example.

As we've already seen, electronic toll collection is a widely accepted new technology for pricing highway access in ways that can mean better mobility for the nation's motorists. It first came on line in the early 1990s as a way to automate the process of collecting tolls without making motorists stop at tollbooths.

Cost-accountant types in the nation's toll authorities quickly saw this as a means of reducing labor costs. By replacing toll collectors with ETC, authorities could attrite down the size of their labor forces over time. This would lead to lower wage bills, smaller pension contributions, less spending for medical insurance and other employee benefits. All costs that had been rising due to inflation and had been expected to continue rising in the future. Adopting ETC would reverse this ever-increasing labor cost spiral.

But this isn't working smarter. It's simply doing the obvious. Even the big three auto manufacturers (whose current financial statements show them to be something less than ace managers) take advantage of opportunities to replace labor with machinery to save money.

Meanwhile, operating managers in these toll authorities saw ETC as a way to streamline their operations. It would allow them to scrap tollbooths entirely, thereby eliminating the bottlenecks caused by long lines of motorists inching slowly forward to stop and pay tolls. The end of such bottlenecks would mean more vehicle throughput per hour – one of the classic engineering measures of how well a roadway is operating.

This isn't working smarter either. It's just another case of doing the obvious.

At the same time, financial types in these authorities realized that the most practical way to implement ETC would be to require motorists to establish pre-payment accounts against which their tolls could be charged. With these accounts having prescribed minimum balances that would be maintained automatically by charging the motorists' credit cards. The financial types could then invest the large cash float from these balances (which technically belong to motorists, but how many of them know that?) in the overnight credit markets to earn interest income for their operations.

Nor is this working smarter. It's simply another variation of the age-old practice among financial types of earning interest for themselves from other people's money.

Fortunately, a few transportation visionaries are coming to see ETC as a way to create a new and more productive relationship between roadway operators and their customers. They're already aware of the cost-saving benefits that ETC offers. And its huge potential for making roadway systems self-supporting by providing new revenues from motorist user charges. These are obvious enough.

But what really matters to these visionaries is how new ETC technology gives transportation managers the ability to use differential pricing to allocate daily travel demand throughout an entire roadway system in the most rational and efficient manner. Doing this means better service for motorists. Even to the extent of operators being able to assure motorists of certain minimum travel speeds if they pay to use toll lanes to speed up their trips. With money-back guarantees if the operators fail to deliver. No questions asked.

Options like this make motorists feel less like members of a captive proletariat and more like free-to-choose customers shopping in a big department store. This changes the whole relationship between motorists and operators in positive ways.

This is what we mean by working smarter.

Let's not forget that people don't buy personal computers by the millions because they want to make contemporary fashion statements in their homes, or impress their friends by using geeky terms like RAM and CPU. They buy because they want to be able to do certain things. Like type letters or reports, crunch numbers, or surf the Internet. And personal computers make this possible.

The same principle can enable us to make transportation better by using new technology in smart ways.

Conclusion: Getting There

In his book *Fooled by Randomness: The Hidden Role of Chance in Life and in the Markets*, securities trader and probability maven Nassim Nicholas Taleb reminds us of something very important:

Just because we've never seen a black swan doesn't automatically mean that all swans are white.

Past experience can all too easily lull us into a false sense of security about how the world works. But the past is only a reliable guide to what's already happened. It tells us little about what can happen in the future. Because black swans are more likely than we might think.

This chapter describes the book's conclusions. In the process, it provides a framework for translating the Driving Questions about the future of transportation in America into a cohesive set of policies, goals and objectives, strategies and tactics, and performance measures to ensure that the approaches being used are effective in achieving the surface transportation vision for the future.

Summing Up

The United States can't realize its full potential in economic, quality of life, and security terms unless its residents and business firms have free-flowing transportation systems capable of handling our growing appetite for mobility and accessibility.

As an open society that values competitive enterprise and individual opportunity, good mobility and accessibility help enhance our freedom to expand employment, housing, and recreation opportunities. Efficient transportation also keeps the nation competitive in the global economy by improving productivity, which boosts prosperity.

Throughout history, most successful nations have enjoyed superior transportation on land and by sea. Indeed, the growth of the United States could not have occurred at the pace it did over the last 230 years without continuous expansion and upgrading of its public and private transportation facilities.

The early turnpikes, canals, and riverboats gave way to steam railroads that knitted the continental United States together. During the early years of the 20th century, electric interurban railways linked growing cities with their surrounding towns. More recently, the Interstate Highway System integrated the lower 48 states into an economic union that offered better opportunities for distribution of goods and people on demand.

Each of these technological steps involved a process of transition from one group of transportation modes to another. The pace of this transition depended on the ability of each mode to meet the overall demand to move people and goods at prices that people were willing to pay.

The United States has been accused of having a "love affair with the automobile." So it seems ironic that the roadways on which motor vehicles depend for movement have received so little support from motorists, who have left them in today's sorry state. But perhaps that's because our love affair is with the automobile itself, which we can customize to our personal needs. It doesn't extend to roadways that (like consumers in the Soviet Union) we have to take or leave in whatever form Big Brother decides to provide.

Government transportation agencies tend to regard the nation's standardized, publicly owned system of roads, bridges, and tunnels as a God-given oil field to be pumped dry with little concern for the future. While the fragmented array of state and local government bureaucracies responsible for its care see it as an inconvenient stepchild.

For the most part, motorists can use roadways without being charged admission fees – just as if they were tax-supported municipal parks or swimming pools. This means that the agencies responsible for them lack the resources to keep pace with the unbridled, price-free demand to travel on them.

The inevitable result is under-maintained, over-used, badly congested roadways that are daily torments for the frustrated motorists who travel on them. Motorists may want free-flowing, showroom-new roadways. But they've come to accept poor quality roadways as an unavoidable result of growth in population, economic activity, and travel.

Hence we may love the privately owned automobile. But we've come to hate the publicly owned highway.

In other words, individual motorists buy and pay for automobiles made by privately owned auto manufacturers that are pushed by competitive pressures to seek ways to constantly improve the cost-effectiveness of their vehicles. But motorists are handed without charge a roadway system largely owned by government agencies that are neither competitive nor innovative, are tied to outdated and inefficient methods, and are administered without any sense of accountability to customers.

Many years ago, someone asked the humorist Will Rogers for a solution to the traffic congestion problems in Los Angeles. His answer was, "Have the government make the cars and the private sector make the roads."

Given the position we're now in, the challenge to develop solutions is both a public sector and private sector responsibility. The VII technology program and the various PPP project financing and delivery initiatives now being applied by selected state and local governments clearly demonstrate the benefits of such cooperation. The key is to find the proper balance of roles, responsibilities, risks, and returns between public and private participants.

This is one of the challenges we must meet in crafting a new vision for surface transportation in America. But first we have to determine how our mobility needs are going to change, how much we're willing to pay for transportation improvements, and who's going to take responsibility for making it all happen. And happen in an expeditious and cost-effective manner that is ultimately responsive to transportation customers: the traveling public, freight carriers, and shippers.

The main conclusions of this book derive from the very questions that prompted its writing:

- **What is the current status of our surface transportation system?**
- **What is our vision for where we want to be in the next 20 to 30 years?**
- **What do we need to start doing, keep doing, and stop doing in the next 5 to 15 years to lay the foundations for realizing this vision?**
- **What do we need to start doing, keep doing, and stop doing over the next 15 to 20 years to carry out this vision?**
- **How do we adapt our vision to changes in domestic**

demographics, competitive global economics, domestic values, and technological advances?

Next Steps

As the chart on the right demonstrates, the next steps involve developing policies and their statutory bases, strategic goals and objectives, and tactical actions that have performance criteria for accountability built into their execution.

Also, this chart illustrates the relationship between defining short-term and long-term visions for transportation, and the development of supporting policies, strategies, and tactics to bring such visions to life.

Policy Focus

- We need a long-range vision of surface transportation that considers all modes for moving people and goods, as well as institutional stakeholders and customers. It must provide maximum opportunity to achieve mutually beneficial synergies among these groups to maximize transportation accessibility, mobility, and productivity for all Americans.

- We should use the next Congressional reauthorization process to focus the surface transportation program on areas of greatest federal interest and responsibility. Motor vehicle fuel taxes will probably continue to generate significant (if increasingly inadequate) revenues for the next 10-to-15 years before the eventual replacement of fossil

VISION TO TACTICS HIERARCHY

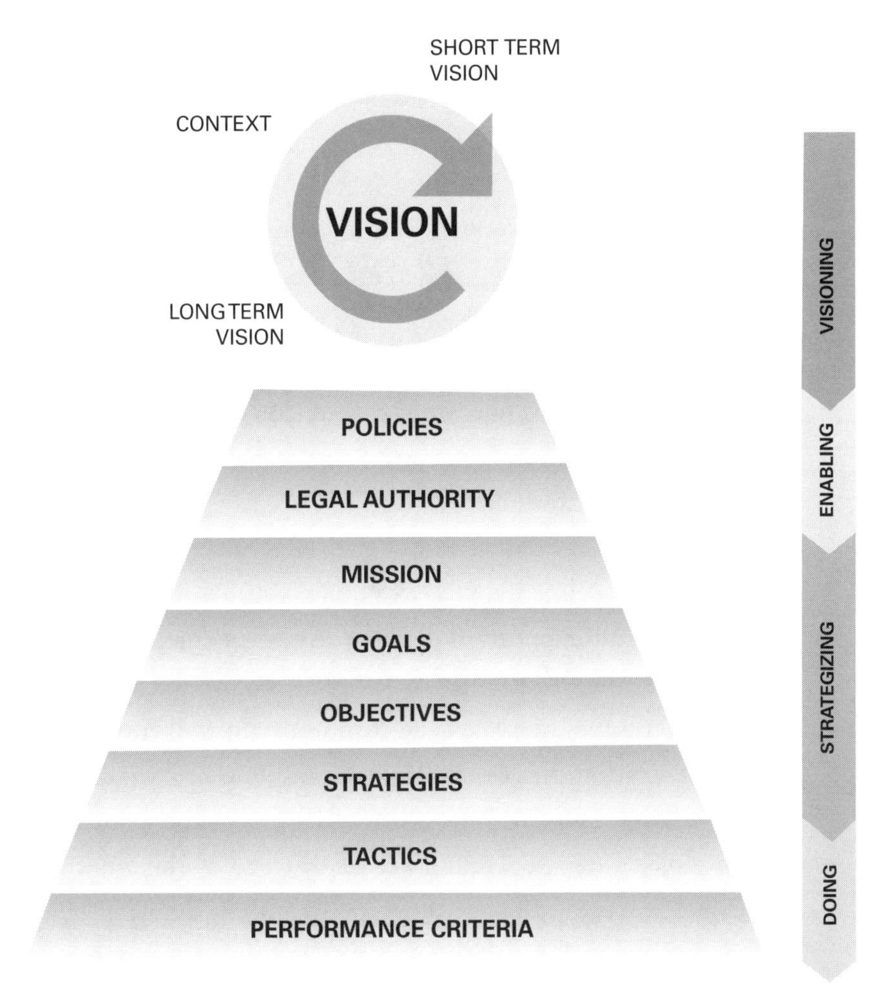

fuel engines diminishes their fiscal capability below the level of relevancy. So federal fuel tax revenues can be a useful supplement to new and more robust revenue sources during the coming decade. But we can no longer depend on them as a funding mainstay.

- The existing federal program should be scrapped as obsolete. We need to replace it with an entirely new program that concentrates federal activities on transportation facilities of clear national interest. These include the existing Interstate Highway System, plus certain other highways of national significance that should become part of a reconstituted Interstate and Cross-Border Highway System. This will require an entirely new approach to Congressional authorization. Not a continuation of the current "creeping incrementalism" approach.

- We need a parallel process to develop an entirely new surface transportation program that can be implemented after the next reauthorization act expires in 2016. There's no point in continuing to tweak the current program through a reauthorization process that's clearly failing in its purpose. We can do this by using the next 10 years to come up with a replacement program that's ready to go by the time the 2009 Surface Transportation program expires. This will provide an orderly transition from the current program (whose revenue sources are becoming increasingly anemic) to a new program that's more relevant, responsible, and flexible in addressing the nation's surface transportation needs during the next 20 to 30 years.

The key feature of the new program should be a soundly conceived vision of surface transportation in America. One that involves all major stakeholders and relies on 21st-century funding, financing, technology and management approaches for a new-generation Interstate and Cross Border Highway System, for safety promotion programs that people can take seriously, for up-to-date technical and research support, and for program quality assurances that define the primary interests of the federal government.

Responsibility and funding for the rest of the program (involving specific roadways and public transportation systems) should be shifted to state and local governments. It should involve all key stakeholders and have broad flexibility to apply innovative techniques for program and project planning, funding and financing, development and delivery, operations, management, preservation, accountability, and program oversight. Cross-subsidies between highway and transit modes would occur at the state and local levels, with priorities determined by these governments.

The new program should be ready by 2016 to completely replace the current program as reauthorized in 2009 (or possibly in 2010 or 2011 if the recent past is any guide).

Strategic Focus

The major barrier to "fixing" the nation's surface transportation program is institutional inertia and opposition by those stakeholders who most benefit from the status quo.

There's no shortage of new ideas for more effective transportation financing, engineering, management, operations, and technology. Such ideas are widely available and rapidly improving. But they can't be implemented while the status quo continues. Institutional inertia is an anchor limiting their use. It can be reduced by lowering the threshold of resistance to change among sponsoring agencies and other traditional program stakeholders. This can be done by making them aware of:

- The advantages to them of having a wider menu of options.
- Emphasizing steps they are comfortable with.
- The expected benefits to them of selected options.
- The negative consequences of failed experimentation are less harmful than they imagine.
- The negative consequences of failing to experiment are more harmful than they imagine.
- The fact that change is the only constant in the world, and resistance to change will ensure they are on their way to becoming obsolete and irrelevant.

We need to recognize that modally fragmented approaches to policy, planning, funding, and operational integration produce poor results for all concerned. But cooperative efforts among transportation stakeholders can result in synergistic benefits for all concerned. Such efforts should include using the marketplace to regulate the balance among stakeholders and modes rather than relying on the Big Brother Command and Control approach of heavy-handed government regulation. Constitutional mandates that the Federal government promote interstate commerce and protect national security should be used to encourage greater innovation and responsibility among state and local governments. Not as excuses to impose heavy handed controls from Washington.

Federal leadership needs to be a major catalyst for replacing the entire program. This is especially important for promoting widespread application of such new approaches and tools as:

- Evolving technologies that facilitate the use of pricing mechanisms to ease congestion, improve the operating capacity of available facilities, and generate badly needed new revenues.

- Promoting competition among providers of highway program services.

- Installing incentives to apply best business practices to such program elements as life-cycle asset management, long-term debt and equity financing, intermodal integration, fund sharing, and customer service.

Tactical Focus

A portfolio of funding, financing, and delivery approaches should be available for state and local transportation agencies to apply in ways that reflect the specific characteristics of each. This would be a marked departure from the current program, which has traditionally relied on a single funding source (motor vehicle fuel taxes), a single financing approach (pay-as-you-build), and a single delivery method (design-bid-build). Such a portfolio approach is being used by state government in Texas to boost its ability to implement major portions of its ambitious Trans-Texas Corridors program.

Based on the results of this research, the following chart shows the key elements of the vision of surface transportation in America:

Closing Remarks

My last book on the state of surface transportation in America noted that a

> *"visionary approach to creating an integrated surface transportation system poses major new financial, technological, and management challenges. But an efficient, well-maintained surface transportation system is a vital element of maintaining national economic competitiveness in a world where the value of saving time and money grows by leaps and bounds. Because these radical changes are likely to take a generation to work their way through the surface transportation system, the time to begin is now."*[43]

The book now in your hands provides both a context and a candid discussion of the challenges facing the providers and users of the nation's surface transportation system to demonstrate the extent of what lies ahead to fix the current system. It underscores the urgency of first developing a comprehensive vision for transforming the surface transportation system in America during the next 20 to 30 years. One that reflects the concerns of all stakeholders and is supported by policies that provide a proper framework for realizing this vision.

Only then can we determine the necessary program goals and objectives, then proceed to develop strategies and tactics to achieve them in ways that turn our vision into reality.

So I conclude with a summary of the Driving Questions that we need to answer in the course of defining this vision:

- What surface transportation capabilities do we need to support the nation's growing population, economy, and standard of living, and to enhance its competitive position in the global economy?

- What aspects of the current surface transportation program should be changed, replaced, and continued to achieve these capabilities in the most cost-effective manner?

- What roles should the public and private sectors play to help achieve these capabilities in a self-sustaining, responsive, and flexible manner that balances responsibilities, risks, and rewards among the participating stakeholder groups?

- How can the diverse components of the nation's surface transportation system be re-engineered to incorporate best practice approaches in funding and financing, facility and service delivery, operations and management, and exploiting new technology?

Fifty years ago, the Interstate Highway System and the age of containerization were born. The first was the work of the public sector, while the second was a private-sector undertaking.

Today, the container shipping business is booming around the world because of its continuing emphasis on raising customer productivity and lowering costs. But the Interstate program has lost momentum in terms of revenue production, service delivery, and innovative use of new technology because it has become bogged down by bureaucracy and antiquated thinking. Despite efforts to rejuvenate the surface transportation program through the Congressional reauthorization process, the changes have been too incremental to forestall the program's decline.

But perhaps federal, state, and local transportation agencies can learn a few things from the example of how the containerization revolution has succeeded. This example includes:

- Start with a basic idea that offers dramatic improvements in productivity and performance while lowering costs.

- Demonstrate the benefits of new approaches or technologies to traditional stakeholders and the negative consequences of continuing the status quo.

- Enable the program to evolve over time and to adapt to changes in technology, customer needs, partners, and market opportunities.

- Standardize interoperability across modes, while allowing standards to be updated as technology and capabilities develop.

- Minimizing Big Brother mandates and prescriptive requirements in order to encourage innovation, creativity, and performance-based rewards among transportation providers.

- Allow time for transition from the current program to what will ultimately augment and replace it.

- Integrate different stakeholder groups into new alliances that can leverage resources and multiply results.

Without seriously overhauling the system to respond to 21st-century needs, we'll wind up singing along with, Bob Dylan:

Hey Mr. Tambourine Man,
Play a song for me.
I'm not sleepy
And there is no place I'm going to.
Hey Mr. Tambourine Man,
Play a song for me.
In the jingle-jangle morning
I'll come following you.

Let's hope it doesn't turn into our new anthem as we sit here stuck in traffic. ■

Appendix A – Road Pricing Terms

ROAD PRICING: An umbrella phrase that covers all direct charges imposed on those who use roadways including fixed tolls and charges that vary with the time of day, the specific road used, and vehicle size and weight.

TOLL WAYS: A road, bridge, or tunnel where motorists are charged a fee according to a fixed schedule.

MANAGED LANES: A lane or lanes designed and operated to achieve stated goals by managing access via user group, pricing or other criteria.

EXPRESS LANES: A set of lanes physically separated from the general-purpose lanes provided within major roadway corridors. Express lane access is managed by limiting the number of entrance and exit points to the facility.

CONGESTION PRICING: The policy of charging drivers a fee that varies by time of day on a fixed schedule (value pricing) or with the level of traffic (dynamic pricing) on a congested roadway. Congestion pricing is designed to allocate roadway space, a scarce resource, in a more economically feasible manner.

TRUCK TOLL WAYS: Truck toll ways consist of one or more lanes in each direction for sole use by trucks, separated from existing lanes by concrete barriers, and generally equipped with their own ingress and egress ramps. May involve variable or dynamic pricing during periods of higher congestion.

VALUE-PRICED EXPRESS LANES: Value pricing uses monetary incentives to manage congestion during peak travel periods. Tolls may be set "dynamically," i.e., they may be increased or decreased every few minutes to manage demand so as to ensure that the express lanes are fully utilized, yet remain uncongested.

HIGH-OCCUPANCY TOLL (HOT) LANES: Managed, limited-access, often barrier-separated highway lanes that provide free or reduced cost access to HOVs, and also make excess capacity available to other vehicles not meeting occupancy requirements at a fixed or market price.

FAST AND INTERTWINED REGULAR (FAIR) LANES: FAIR lanes divide currently free, general-purpose traffic lanes into tolled express lanes that limit traffic to the free-flowing maximum and more congested, but free, regular lanes where drivers are compensated with credits that could be used as toll payments on days when they choose to use express lanes.

CORDON PRICING: Cordon tolls are fees paid by motorists who cross a cordon line or drive in a particular cordon area, usually a city center. Some cordon tolls only apply during peak periods, such as weekdays.

DYNAMIC PRICING: Tolls that vary in real time in response to changing congestion levels as opposed to variable pricing that follows a fixed schedule.

VALUE PRICING: A concept that uses monetary incentives to manage congestion during peak travel periods on tolled highways and crossing facilities.

Source:
Various Sources of Road Pricing Terms
FHWA definition
Texas A & M
Eno Transportation Foundation
TDM Encyclopedia
Reason Public Policy Institute

Appendix B – Definitions of Alternative PPP Arrangements

Contracting Method	Major Features of Contracting Method
raditional Design-Bid-Build ontract	Public agency designs the project and awards construction contract to private sector. Very little opportunity for innovation or efficiencies.
+B Contracting	This is a modification of the traditional design, bid, build contract in which the private contractor bids both the project cost (A) and the time to complete the project (B). The contractor assumes the risk of not completing the project in the specified time, and bonuses for early completion or penalties for late completion typically are included.
aintenance Contract	This type of contract is used for long-term maintenance and/or operation of an existing facility or system of facilities. The private sector typically would be responsible for financing needed improvements and would be paid a fee by the public sector for doing so. The fee may include performance incentives or disincentives. Experience to date is that private sector management contracts can often result in substantial cost savings over traditional public sector management of the road system.
esign-Build Contract	The private sector is given the responsibility for design and construction of the facility. This promotes innovation in design and efficiencies in the construction process since the same firm or group of firms are responsible for both design and construction.
esign-Build Contract with arranty	In addition to giving the private sector the responsibility to design and construct the facility, the private sector provides a warranty for key components of the project (from 5 to 20 years). The private sector may or may not participate in project financing.
sign, Build, Operate, Maintain ntract (concession or nchise)	This is similar to the DBFO contract, but involves a lesser role by the private sector in project finance. Like the DBFO, the private sector assumes major responsibilities for project design, construction methods, operations, and maintenance. Payments from the public sector may include performance incentives/disincentives for operational performance and physical condition.
sign, Build, Finance, Operate, intain Contract (concession or nchise)	Under the DBFO contracting method the private sector is responsible for all or a major part of project financing as well as facility design, construction, operation, and maintenance. Typically the facility reverts to the State after 25+ years. Revenues to the private sector can come from direct user charges, payments from the public sector, or both. Operations typically would be covered by performance incentives, and contracts would have to include such things as maximum rate of return, non-compete clauses, and maximum toll rates, etc.
ild-Operate-Transfer, ild-Transfer-Operate, or ild-Own-Operate Contract	Build-Operate-Transfer/ (BOT)– contract team finances, builds, and operates facility to sponsor specifications until end of contract or franchise term when it transfers to public sponsor. A Build-Transfer-Operate (BTO) team finances and builds facility and transfers to public sponsor at end of construction period, and then leases back the facility to operate until end of contract term. A Build-Own-Operate (BOO) team finances, builds, and operates facility and keeps title to the asset, typically under franchise to public sponsor.
nt Development Project	Formal arrangement whereby private sector developers of property at or near public-use infrastructure share development rights, risks, and rewards with public sector sponsors of infrastructure improvement projects that benefit these developments through improved accessibility.
ely Private Project	There is virtually no involvement by the public sector in the project and no contract or other formal agreement between the public and private sectors. This includes asset sales.

Endnotes

[1]Drucker, Peter F. – *Management: Tasks, Responsibilities, Practices.* New York: Harper & Row, 1973.

[2]Originally attributed to Damon Runyon, New York City newspaperman paraphrasing a verse in Ecclesiastes.

[3]Einstein, Albert. – (1879- 1955) Physicist and Professor, Nobel Prize 1921.

[4]Excerpted from remarks made by Mary Peters at her swearing-in ceremony as the new Secretary of Transportation on October 17, 2006 in Washington, DC.

[5]*Highway Statistics 2005,* Table HF-10. Office of Highway Policy Information, Federal Highway Administration, US DOT. November 2006.

[6]According to the *Clay Commission Report on the National Highway Program* issued in February 1955, there were 5,242 miles of tolled highways operating, under construction, funded, or authorized in the U.S. at the beginning of 1955 (p. 26). This compared to 6,417 miles of non-tolled highways that had been improved by the early 1950s according to the report: *The Road that Built America* by Dan McNichol, published by Sterling Publishing Co., Inc., New York City, NY 2006, p. 102.

[7]From testimony offered by Jeffery Shane, Undersecretary of Transportation for Policy for the USDOT at the second meeting of the National Surface Transportation Policy and Revenue Study Commission, held in Washington, D.C. on June 26, 2006.

[8]*The Intermodal Container Era, History, Security, and Trends.* TR NEWS, Number 246, Transportation Research Board of the National Academies, Washington, D.C., September-October 2006, pp. 5-23.

[9]*Table 3 – Transportation and the U.S. Economy.* Bureau of Transportation Statistics. Year 2001 for GDP and Year 2002 for employment statistics, October 13, 2006.

[10]Drawn in part from testimony given to the National Surface Transportation Policy and Revenue Study Commission by Joseph M. Giglio, Ph.D. College of Business Administration – Center for Strategic Studies, Northeastern University on October 9, 2006 titled *Unanswered Questions: Developing a National Transportation Strategy.*

[11]Ibid.

[12]Arthur C. Nelson, Metropolitan Institute at Virginia Tech, as reported in the article: *Where will everybody live?* **USA TODAY,** October 27, 2006, pp. 1A-2A.

[13]Stambrook, David. Chapter 4 – Key *Factors Driving the Future Demand for Surface Transport Infrastructure and Services.* Infrastructure to 2030 – Telecom, Land, Transport, Water and Electricity. OEDC Publishing, ISBN 92-64-02398-4, May 2006. p. 192.

[14]From testimony offered by Jack Wells, Senior Economist for the USDOT at the second meeting of the National Surface Transportation Policy and Revenue Study Commission, held in Washington, D.C. on June 26, 2006.

[15]*2010 and Beyond – A Vision of America's Transportation Future – Chapter 1: Current Outlook for Transportation Finance.* The Hudson Institute, 2004, p. 23.

[16]Balaker, Ted. *Why Mobility Matters.* Reason Foundation Policy Brief No. 43, Los Angeles, CA. August 2006.

[17]*Value Pricing Project Quarterly Report – July – September 2006.* Office of Operations Division, Federal Highway Administration, Washington, D.C. September 2006.

[18]*How Technology Can Help Us Avoid Traffic.* Steve Svekis, Sun-Sentinel, September 23, 2006.

[19] Surface Transportation Program and Finance History .... From testimony offered by Jack Basso to the National Surface Transportation Policy and Revenue Study Commission, AASHTO, August 2006.

[20]*2010 and Beyond – A Vision of America's Transportation Future – Chapter 1: Current Outlook for Transportation Finance.* The Hudson Institute, 2004, p. 22.

[21]Office of Planning and Environment, Federal Transit Administration, US DOT Washington, D.C., November, 2006.

[22]*Fuel Tax and Alternatives for Transportation Funding – TRB Special Report 285.* Committee for the Study of the Long-Term Viability of Fuel Taxes for Transportation Finance, Transportation Research Board of the National Academies, Washington, D.C., 2006, p. 2.

[23]*GASB Statement No. 34 – Basic Financial Statement – and Management's Discussion and Analysis for State and Local Governments.* Governmental Accounting Standards Board. Norwalk, CT., June 1999.

[24]*NCHRP Report 522 – A Review of DOT Compliance with GASB 34 Requirements.* Sponsored research by the American Association of State Highway and Transportation Officials and the Federal Highway Administration through the National Cooperative Highway Research Program of the Transportation Research Board, Washington, D.C., 2004.

[25]Issues and Options for Increasing the Use of Tolling and Pricing to Finance Transportation Improvements. AECOM Consult, Inc. for FHWA's Office of Transportation Policy Studies, June 2006. p. 4-11.

[26]Keegan, John. Chapter 6 – *The First World War.* Knopf Publishing, May, 1999.

[27]Drucker, Peter F. – *The Effective Executive.* HaperCollins Publishers, April 1993.

[28]Adapted from the title to Joseph M. Giglio's recent book: MOBILITY – America's Transportation Mess and How to Fix It. Hudson Institute, Washington, D.C., 2005.

[29]As suggested by Kenneth Orski in his Innovation Briefs Commentary – *Thinking About the Future of Federal Transit Investment,* September 14, 2006.

[30]Stambrook, David. Chapter 4 – Key *Factors Driving the Future Demand for Surface Transportation Infrastructure and Services.* Infrastructure to 2030 – Telecom, Land, Transport, Water and Electricity. OEDC Publishing, ISBN 92-64-02398-4, May 2006, p. 217.

[31]Giglio, Joseph M. *Mobility: All Roads Lead to Texas.* Keynote address presented to the Texas Transportation Forum, Austin, Texas, June 8, 2006. Excerpted from the Future of Transportation Finance issue of Horizon. *The Future of Transportation* published by the Texas Department of Transportation, Summer 2006, pp 57-61. The Regional Mobility Corporation or RMC organizational concept was developed by Joseph M. Giglio, Ph.D., a professor of Strategic Management at the Graduate School of Business, Northeastern University.

[32]*Report to Congress on Public-Private Partnerships.* United States Department of Transportation, Federal Highway Administration, December 2004.

[33]Federal Highway Administrator Mary Peters address at the inaugural PPP workshop entitled: "Partnerships for Transportation and Real Estate: A Union Station Anniversary". Held at Union Station in Washington, D.C., September 24, 2003.

[34]*Voters Back All Major Transportation-Related Ballot Initiatives Nationwide.* Press Release by the American Association of Sate Highway and Transportation Officials (AASHTO). Washington, D.C., November 8, 2006.

[35]*Implementing the VII Vision: Lessons from the Past.* College of Business Administration, Northeastern University. September 9, 2005, pp. 9-10.

[36]Ibid, p. 2

[37]*The Brave New World of Vehicle Infrastructure Integration: Transforming Transportation As We Know It.* College of Business Administration, Northeastern University, August 31, 2005, pp. 36-66.

[38]*Nissan to Test Intelligent Transportation System in Kanagawa – Advanced Road Traffic System Aimed at Reducing Accidents, Easing Congestion.* Nissan News Press Release, September 15, 2006.

[39]*BMW to Offer Better Traffic Information,* PC Magazine, October 12, 2006.

[40]*RCI and CESARE IIII Join Forces.* ERTICO News Release, September 16, 2006.

[41]*Trucks Morph into High-Tech Networks on 18 Wheels – Onboard Software and Wireless Communications Combine to Give Owners Unprecedented Visibility into their Truck Fleets.* Charles Babcock, InformationWeek, September 25, 2006.

[42]http://en.wikipedia.org/wiki//Highway_407_(Ontario)

[43]Giglio, Joseph M. MOBILITY – America's Transportation Mess and How to Fix It. Hudson Institute, Washington, D.C., 2005, p. 301.

Bibliography

2010 and Beyond: A Vision of America's Transportation Future, Chapter 1, "Current Outlook for Transportation Finance," (Washington, D.C.: The Hudson Institute, 2004).

AECOM Consult, Inc. *Issues and Options for Increasing the Use of Tolling and Pricing to Finance Transportation Improvements.* FHWA's Office of Transportation Policy Studies, June 2006, p. 4-11.

Balaker, Ted. *Why Mobility Matters.* Reason Foundation Policy Brief No. 43, Los Angeles, CA, August 2006.

Babcock, Charles. "Trucks Morph into High-Tech Networks on 18 Wheels – Onboard Software and Wireless Communications Combine to Give Owners Unprecedented Visibility into their Truck Fleets." *InformationWeek* September 25, 2006.

"BMW to Offer Better Traffic Information." *PC* Magazine, October 12, 2006.

Damon, Runyon. New York City newspaperman paraphrasing a verse in Ecclesiastes.

Drucker, Peter F. *The Effective Executive* (New York: HaperCollins Publishers, 1993).

GASB Statement No. 34 – Basic Financial Statement – and Management's Discussion and Analysis for State and Local Governments. Governmental Accounting Standards Board. Norwalk, CT., June 1999.

Giglio, Joseph M. *Mobility: America's Transportation Mess and How to Fix It* (Washington, D.C.: Hudson Institute, 2005).

Keegan, John. *The First World War* (New York: Knopf, 1999).

McFarland, Stephen L. *America's Pursuit of Precision Bombing, 1910-1945,* (TK: Smithsonian Institution Press, 1995).

McNichol, Dan. *The Road That Built America* (New York: Sterling Publishing Co., 2006).

Miller, Donald L. *Masters of the Air: America's Bomber Boys Who Fought the Air War Against Nazi Germany* (New York: Simon & Schuster, 2006).

Nelson, Arthur C. "Where will everybody live?" *USA Today*. Metropolitan Institute at Virginia Tech. October 27, 2006, pp. 1A-2A.

"Nissan to Test Intelligent Transportation System in Kanagawa: Advanced Road Traffic System Aimed at Reducing Accidents, Easing Congestion." Nissan News Press Release, September 15, 2006.

Northeastern University, College of Business. *Implementing the VII Vision: Lessons from the Past*. September 9, 2005.

Northeastern University, College of Business. *The Brave New World of Vehicle Infrastructure Integration: Transforming Transportation As We Know It*. August 31, 2005.

Office of Highway Policy Information, Federal Highway Administration. *Highway Statistics 2005*. U.S. DOT. November 2006.

Paton, Dean. "Your Personal Toll Booth," *Washington CEO* Magazine. October 31, 2006.

"RCI and CESARE IIII Join Forces," *ERTICO* News Release. September 16, 2006.

Stambrook, David. *Infrastructure to 2030: Telecom, Land, Transport, Water and Electricity. Key Factors Driving the Future Demand for Surface Transport Infrastructure and Services*. (OEDC Publishing, 2006).

Svekis, Steve. "How Technology Can Help Us Avoid Traffic." *Orlando Sun-Sentinel*. September 23, 2006.

Taleb, Nassim Nicholas. *Fooled by Randomness: The Hidden Role of Chance in Life and the Markets* (New York: Random House, 2005).

The Intermodal Container Era, History, Security, and Trends. TR News, Number 246, Transportation Research Board of the National Academies, Washington, D.C., September-October 2006, pp. 5-23.

World Wide Web. Wikipedia. 407 Express Toll Route (ETR). <http:en.wikipedia.org/wiki/Highway_407_(Ontario).